I0762708

TO

FROM

DATE

Hope in the Hard

INTERACTIVE INSPIRATIONAL JOURNAL

You're Not Alone

You're imperfect, and you're wired for struggle, but you are worthy of love and belonging.

BRENÉ BROWN

Life is messy. The struggles are real and can be a punch in the gut at times. There are days when you wish you could stay in bed with the covers pulled over your head. (Please, Lord?) Well-meaning friends try to coax you back to the sunlight, but all you can see is the rain, so you resign yourself to the notion that things are never going to get better. (Boo! Hiss!)

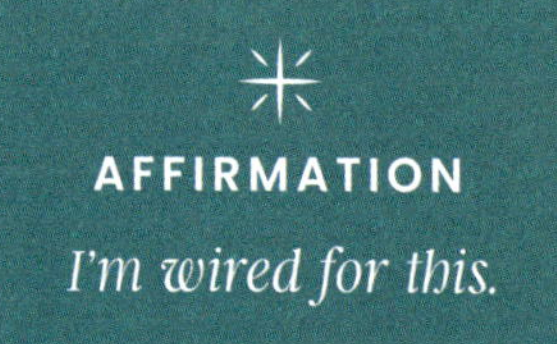

Then—gasp!—you realize you're not alone. Seated in the cubicle next to you at work is a gal who just lost her husband. You can see the heartache resonating in her tear-filled eyes. And in another cubicle not far away, an elderly coworker has just received a cancer diagnosis. The weariness in her voice cuts to the heart.

You squint to see your boss as he passes through the room. He's on his cell phone, angry with someone on the other end of the line. He ends the call with an exaggerated groan.

Would hollering, "Been there, done that!" be inappropriate?

Your thoughts begin to shift. On some weird level, knowing you're not the only one struggling helps.

You rise and take a few steps toward the coworker dealing with the cancer diagnosis. Her slumped shoulders reflect the weight of what she's carrying. Her red-rimmed eyes are puffy. You take a seat next to her and whisper, "You're not going to go through this alone, I promise." She takes your hand and gives it a squeeze, then glances your way with a glimmer of hope in her eyes.

As you make your way back to your seat, the Lord echoes those same words back to your heart: "You're going to make it through this. The answers might not come today. They might not come tomorrow. But you are wired for this, and things will eventually get better. There are brighter days ahead. No, really."

GOD SAYS

"Fear not, for I am with you; be not dismayed, for I am your God; I will strengthen you, I will help you, I will uphold you with my righteous right hand."

ISAIAH 41:10 ESV

TRUTH FOR TODAY

You don't have to face this situation alone because the God of the universe is with you.

REFLECTION

I might feel like I'm trekking through the valley completely alone, but God's Word specifically promises me that . . .

"FOR *I know the plans* I HAVE FOR YOU,"

SAYS THE LORD.

"THEY ARE PLANS FOR *good*

AND NOT FOR DISASTER,

TO GIVE YOU *a future and a hope.*"

JEREMIAH 29:11 NLT

ACTIVITY

Circle all that are true.

God takes naps.

No one else is going through what I'm going through.

God cares.

The world is filled with people who feel just like me.

God is hiding from me.

God is omnipresent.

Jesus understands how I'm feeling.

I should give in to feelings of loneliness.

His presence is real.

God is with me wherever I go.

Shimmers of Light

I will love the light for it shows me the way,
yet I will endure the darkness for it shows me the stars.

OG MANDINO

You've done all the right things. But the situation still isn't resolving. In fact, it's getting worse by the moment. Ugh. Well-meaning friends spout the adage, "When you reach the end of your rope, tie a knot and hang on!" but you want to slug them. (Would that be wrong?) Right now, you're too exhausted to remember how to tie a knot. Do they really think sugarcoated platitudes will help?

These impossible situations spin into your life like unexpected meteors and threaten to take you down. But God wants to remind you today that He's in the hope business. There are shimmers of light, even in the darkest situations. If you look for them, you will surely find them. And when you do, those little hope beacons can change everything.

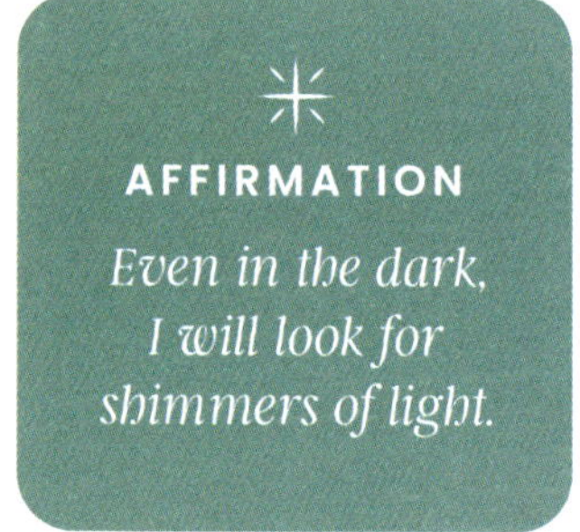

Kendra experienced this firsthand. When her daughter Jenna was hospitalized with cystic fibrosis, Kendra nearly lost her ability to hang on. Between her job, the daily trips back and forth to the hospital, and plenty of chaos from her other three kids, hope nearly slipped out the window. But then, in the middle of the struggle, something rather miraculous occurred. Jenna made friends with another girl she shared a hospital room with. In fact, the two became so close that Jenna cried on the day she had to leave the hospital. They vowed to remain close, to never lose touch. And they kept that promise.

They are teensy-tiny things, these shimmers, but they are mammoth when you glance in the rearview mirror years later. Little beacons of light bring hope and whisper, "Hang on! Don't give up!" They shift your focus upward, away from the situation and toward the One who is big enough to manage it.

What impossible circumstances are you facing today? Look up! Stars are twinkling overhead, begging you to remember that hope can still be found, even in the impossible.

GOD SAYS

So we do not lose heart. Though our outer self is wasting away, our inner self is being renewed day by day. For this light momentary affliction is preparing for us an eternal weight of glory beyond all comparison, as we look not to the things that are seen but to the things that are unseen. For the things that are seen are transient, but the things that are unseen are eternal.

II CORINTHIANS 4:16–18 ESV

TRUTH FOR TODAY

Hope is a radiant shimmer of light in an otherwise-dark season.

REFLECTION

I refuse to lose heart during difficult seasons
because God's Word promises me . . .

"WHEN YOU PASS THROUGH THE WATERS,
I will be with you; AND WHEN
YOU PASS THROUGH THE RIVERS,
THEY WILL *not sweep over you.*
WHEN YOU WALK THROUGH THE FIRE,
YOU WILL *not be burned*;
THE FLAMES WILL NOT SET YOU ABLAZE.
For I am the LORD your God."

ISAIAH 43:2–3 NIV

ACTIVITY

Write a poem using the letters from the phrase below.

H ____________________

O ____________________

P ____________________

E ____________________

I ____________________

N ____________________

H ____________________

I ____________________

M ____________________

When Life Gives You Lemons

Start by doing what's necessary; then do what's possible;
and suddenly you are doing the impossible.

FRANCIS OF ASSISI

You didn't ask for it. You don't feel like you deserve it. And you're most assuredly not feeling up to making lemonade out of it. But life has given you another lemon to add to the ever-growing pile, and you'd like to give it a swift kick back to where it came from. You're done. Finished. Kaput. One unfair circumstance after another has tried to knock your knees out from under you. You're beginning to wonder if there's some sort of target on your forehead. There's certainly one on your heart. These things you're facing are unjust. They're downright cruel, in fact.

You've moaned. You've groaned. You've turned multiplied choruses of "Why me, Lord?" into your swan song, and you're now ready to give an encore. But those sour lemons keep flying your way as more inequities come. They pile up around your feet at the office as you face ongoing issues with your boss. (Really? You're accusing me of not doing my fair share? I work harder than anyone else here!) They seem to pelt you when the kids get home from school. (Are these kids of mine going to hate each other forever?) And they threaten to drown you when you attempt to pay the bills. (More month than money . . . again?) How is any of this fair?

AFFIRMATION

Life doesn't have to be fair to be full.

It's easy to grow bitter when life is unjust. But there's something to be said for that old expression about turning lemons into lemonade. You can't always control what comes. But with God's help, you can sweeten the taste by inviting Him into the situation. You might not notice the change in taste right away, but if you'll shift your perspective even a little, He might just surprise you with a tiny sip of goodness, right there in the middle of your pain.

GOD SAYS

"I have said these things to you,
that in me you may have peace.
In the world you will have tribulation.
But take heart; I have overcome the world."

JOHN 16:33 ESV

TRUTH FOR TODAY

Bad things happen, but I can still choose peace.

REFLECTION

I've always looked at "lemon" experiences as bitter, but God's Word reminds me . . .

The Lord is a *refuge* for the oppressed,

a *stronghold* in times of trouble.

Those who know your name *trust in You,*

for You, Lord, have *never forsaken*

those who seek You.

Psalm 9:9–10 NIV

ACTIVITY

Fill in the blanks to remind yourself of the many times God turned your lemons into lemonade.

Numb

By default, most of us have taken the dare to simply survive. Exist. Get through. For the most part, we live numb to life—we've grown weary and apathetic and jaded . . . and wounded.

ANN VOSKAMP

"How are you feeling about all this?"

Megan shrugged in response to her friend's question. How could she possibly put into words what she was feeling? Or not feeling, as the case might be. After all she'd been through over the past several months, the idea of allowing herself to feel seemed like too much.

Megan paused and then sighed. "I think I've lost the ability to feel. I'm just . . . numb. And that's going to have to be okay right now. It's all I can manage."

AFFIRMATION

Today I will dare to feel.

Maybe you can relate. You've been so inundated by the onslaught of attacks that you've constructed massive brick walls to keep out the pain, carefully jabbing mortar into any cracks. You pray those walls will protect your heart, but you can't deny the obvious: they've also blocked out any emotions that might have penetrated the surface and offered some relief. You can't cry. You can't laugh. You can't seem to do much of anything . . . and you've reconciled yourself to that fact. But deep down inside you wonder if things will always be this way.

Let's face it—Novocain is great when you're seated in the dentist's chair, about to undergo a root canal, but it's only meant to be temporary, until the worst of the pain passes. If your mouth remained numb forever, you would have a hard time functioning.

The same is true with your heart. Numb is okay for today. But what happens when we invite the numbness to stick around for weeks, months, or maybe even years? How long should we let it drag on? Could it be that we actually need those feelings in order to survive? Maybe it's time to ask God if there is a reason for the painful feelings. Ask Him to return them to you. Today might be a good day to take a risk and ask, knowing that the One who answers will walk with you through it all.

GOD SAYS

Keep your heart with all vigilance,
for from it flow the springs of life.

PROVERBS 4:23 ESV

TRUTH FOR TODAY

God is faithful, even when I'm not feeling it.

REFLECTION

On those days when everything inside of me feels withered, dry, and numb, I can still . . .

"I KNOW YOUR DEEDS,

THAT YOU ARE

neither cold nor hot.

I WISH YOU WERE EITHER

one or the other!"

REVELATION 3:15 NIV

ACTIVITY

My hard "to-do" list: Ten tasks that seem impossible when I'm feeling numb:

1. ______________________________

2. ______________________________

3. ______________________________

4. ______________________________

5. ______________________________

6. ______________________________

7. ______________________________

8. ______________________________

9. ______________________________

10. ______________________________

Fully Full

My brokenness is a better bridge for people than my pretend wholeness ever was.

SHEILA WALSH

Picture a bicycle. You've ordered it from an online store, and it just arrived at your front door, but it's missing something—the handlebars. Weird.

Imagine a cake. The baker added all the ingredients except one—baking soda. Instead of receiving a light, fluffy concoction, you're presented with a solid lump of baked flour. Ick.

Now envision a brand-new car on the showroom floor. It's ready to go, except that it's only got three wheels. Um, no thank you.

These might seem like odd illustrations, but this is how we view ourselves at times. We feel incomplete, as if we're not enough. We're missing tires. Or handlebars. Or baking soda. And we go through life wondering if we'll ever find the missing parts necessary to feel fully baked (er, whole). It's hard to live a full life when your glass is half-empty, after all.

Oh, but listen! Today, the Lord is whispering to your heart, "You are enough." Allow those words to sink in as you analyze their meaning: "You don't have to do anything or be anything more than what you already are." Your loving heavenly Father finds great value and worth in you, not because of anything you've done, but simply because you're His child. And He wants you to begin to see yourself that way too. Instead of focusing on the missing parts, accept the love that He's offering you, just as you are.

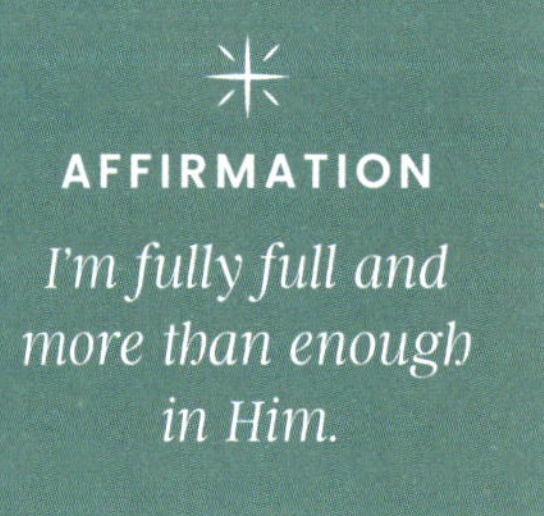

You might be broken. You might be a hot, half-baked mess. But He sees you as beautifully whole and fully full. So, don't miss out on one moment of life or waste too much time looking to complete yourself. In Him, you already are. And boy, does He have amazing plans for all your tomorrows! So hang in there, sister! There are brighter days ahead.

GOD SAYS

So you also are complete
through your union with Christ,
who is the head over
every ruler and authority.

COLOSSIANS 2:10 NLT

TRUTH FOR TODAY

In Him, I am more than enough.

REFLECTION

On the days when I feel like a broken,
half-baked mess, I will remember . . .

I WILL *give thanks to You,*

BECAUSE I AM *awesomely*

AND *wonderfully made;*

wonderful ARE YOUR WORKS,

AND *my soul knows it* VERY WELL.

PSALM 139:14 NASB

ACTIVITY

Some days we feel incomplete, as if we're not enough.
Fill in the blanks below to show how Gods says you are enough!

I FEEL LIKE THIS IS MISSING IN MY LIFE	BUT GOD SAYS

Inside Your Story

Rivers know this: there is no hurry. We shall get there some day.

A. A. MILNE

When an author sits down to write a novel, she creates an exciting cast of characters and gives them a plot filled with breathtaking twists and turns. She creates the perfect setting, one that makes sense to both story and cast. And she somehow merges it all into one lovely tale that keeps you turning page after page.

Each character has a backstory, of course. Those "who he used to be" bits offer the reader bread crumbs . . . clues, if you will. If you know where someone has come from, it's easier to see where he's going, after all.

Still, if you pay close attention, you'll notice a good author doesn't dump in all the character's backstory right away. Tiny snippets of it come out as the plot moves along. This is what keeps you, the reader, interested—all is not revealed at once.

You have a backstory too. You've been through a lot. And God (who happens to be an amazing Author, by the way) isn't spending a lot of time throwing your backstory into your present situation. He's also not throwing it in your face. Sure, it had some fascinating plot points. Yes, it has made you into the person you are. There's no denying some of the places you've been or things you've done. But He is more concerned with today. And tomorrow.

AFFIRMATION

I will not allow my past to define my present or my future.

Maybe you're worried about what other people think about you, based on where you've come from. Remember: they've come from someplace too. And just because you can't see their backstory doesn't mean it's not there. Every person on planet Earth wishes he or she could change certain elements of the past. (If only!) But there's a reason it's called a backstory. It's behind you now. And it's mighty hard to go forward if you keep looking back.

That's what the Lord wants for you, by the way—forward motion. Stepping into a bright future. Trusting Him, in spite of the backstory.

GOD SAYS

And we know that in all things
God works for the good of those who love Him,
who have been called according to His purpose.

ROMANS 8:28 NIV

TRUTH FOR TODAY

Mountains or valleys, good times or bad,
God will use them all
to work something beautiful in my life.

REFLECTION

When I'm down in the valley, I tend to worry,
but the Bible reminds me that . . .

ANYONE WHO

belongs to Christ

HAS BECOME *a new person.*

THE OLD LIFE IS GONE;

A *new life* HAS BEGUN!

2 CORINTHIANS 5:17 NLT

ACTIVITY

Your life has been filled with many highs and lows—mountain peaks and deep valleys! Tell your backstory by writing some of your experiences into the graphic below.

Those Beautiful, Ugly Tears

A diamond is a chunk of coal
that did well under pressure.

HENRY KISSINGER

If you ever want to give yourself a shock, take a peek in the mirror when you're in the middle of a good cry. Ack! Who is that woman staring back at you, the one with the mascara running down her cheeks? The one with her lips tugged down in a frown? You don't recognize her at all! Of course, the puffy eyes aren't helping. They've affected your vision. You can barely see the reflection staring back at you, right?

Becca did her best to avoid the emotions bottled up inside her as she fought the temptation to cry. The season she found herself in had tossed one heartbreak after another her way. She just couldn't seem to catch a break. But releasing the pain? Letting the tears out? She wasn't sure she wanted that dam to break. If it did, would there ever be an end to it, or would she flood the house? So, instead of crying, she forced a smile and forged ahead, determined to power through.

Here's a fun fact about tears: They are cleansing. Refreshing. A visible demonstration of the pain leaking out. And that's a good thing because if you left it inside, you'd be like a volcano, always on the verge of erupting. (That sounds painful!)

AFFIRMATION

"My flesh and my heart may fail, but God is the strength of my heart" (PSALM 73:26 NIV).

Take a good look at today's quote from Henry Kissinger: "A diamond is a chunk of coal that did well under pressure." Crying doesn't mean you're not doing well under pressure. No, really. After all you've been through, a meltdown from time to time is kind of inevitable. And who do you think created those tears, anyway? Remember, the Bible says that even Jesus wept.

So let those tears flow. Get the feelings out. And remember, you can't move into a bright and beautiful tomorrow until you've dealt with the pain of the here and now. Today's cleansing tears will help you step into tomorrow's healthy possibilities.

GOD SAYS

You keep track of all my sorrows.
You have collected all my tears in your bottle.
You have recorded each one in your book.

PSALM 56:8 NLT

TRUTH FOR TODAY

Every pain, every tear has been collected in a bottle by the One who knows me best and loves me most.

REFLECTION

When I finally allow that emotional dam to break, then I'm finally free to . . .

MY FLESH AND MY HEART MAY FAIL,

BUT *God is the strength of my heart.*

PSALM 73:26 ESV

ACTIVITY

Reflect on your most recent painful experience.
How did you feel before releasing the problem to God?
How did you feel after?

BEFORE RELEASING, I FELT . . .

AFTER RELEASING, I FELT . . .

One Dust Bunny at a Time

If you have been harboring anger or bitterness or jealousy in your heart . . . hand it over to Christ, and ask Him to help you let it go.

BILLY GRAHAM

Cindy tidied up her office, ashamed of how messy she'd let it get. How did things pile up like that? Oh, right. When you worked as many hours as she did, it happened.

Exhausted, she finally took a seat at her desk to dive into a work-related spreadsheet. She happened to glance to her right and noticed, under a small table, dust bunnies on the floor, along with a couple of scraps of paper.

Really? How had she managed to overlook some of the mess, in spite of her seemingly thorough cleaning? A change of perspective had revealed the situation, and now she had no choice but to remedy it. The spreadsheet would have to wait.

Maybe you've been there. You've worked on certain areas of your life, tidying up. You've fixed the anger, the bitterness, the lack of self-control. Whew! You think you're all done with the hard work. Then something happens—a friend says something unkind, a child sasses you, your boss corrects you—and Pandora's box is flung open. Unexpectedly harsh words, emotions, and attitudes soar out, zooming toward their intended target.

AFFIRMATION

I will let go of everything that is holding me back from soaring.

Whoa. Where did all that come from? Girl, you've just discovered the hidden clutter under the table, and it must be dealt with. Those dust bunnies have to go!

Why do you suppose God forces us to look at those icky wisps of dust and torn scraps of paper? Because He's got bigger, better things ahead for us. He doesn't want us to get caught up in the debris of the past or the murky shadows of situations that no longer hold us in their grasp. Instead, He wants us freed up to soar, and that can only happen if we take the time to clean up the mess, one dust bunny at a time.

GOD SAYS

Then Peter came up and said to him,
"Lord, how often will my brother sin against me, and I forgive him?
As many as seven times?" Jesus said to him,
"I do not say to you seven times, but seventy-seven times."

MATTHEW 18:21–22 ESV

TRUTH FOR TODAY

I don't always feel like forgiving,
but it's always the right thing to do.

REFLECTION

Seventy-seven times? Really, Lord?
What about how many times he/she has hurt me?
Still, Your Word says . . .

IF THEY FALL,

IT ISN'T FATAL,

FOR *the Lord holds them*

WITH HIS HAND.

PSALM 37:24 TLB

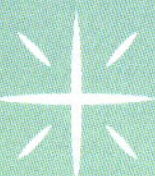

ACTIVITY

How full is your dustpan?
Is there someone you need to forgive?

TODAY I CHOOSE RELEASE FROM . . .

Just Breathe

You can't be brave if you've only had wonderful things happen to you.

MARY TYLER MOORE

Have you ever wondered why women are taught Lamaze breathing techniques for when they're in labor? When the pain is severe, focusing on something else—anything, really—helps. A lot.

In. Out. In. Out.

When you're fixated on the motion of the breaths and your eyes are focused on a single spot on the wall, you're not thinking about the pain.

In theory, anyway.

No doubt life has offered you plenty of laborious moments. Not the kinds that produce a child but the kinds that eventually lead to something beautiful, if you can just press through the pain without panicking or giving up. But that's not always easy in the moment, is it?

Maybe you've heard the expression "Just breathe!" If you're like most people, panic can cause you to literally hold your breath. But don't hold it for long. Even in the middle of a crisis, breathe.

AFFIRMATION

Today I choose to believe that "perfect love casts out fear" (I JOHN 4:18 ESV).

In. Out. In. Out.

Breathing is the answer. When you face a crisis, allow the breath of the Holy Spirit to calm you. He is your Comforter, you know. He's right there, ready to bind up your fears as you focus on Him.

Lynn learned this as she walked through a particularly tough experience with the IRS. A routine audit turned up unfounded accusations on their end, and she nearly panicked. Talk about holding your breath! Lynn got her breathing under control enough to pray about the situation and place it in God's hands. Before long, He pointed her in the direction of a good CPA, who helped her fight back—and win.

There will always be opportunities to panic. But remember, on the other side of the storms you usually find sunny skies and new possibilities. So, don't give up—and don't forget to breathe!

GOD SAYS

"Peace I leave with you; my peace I give to you.
Not as the world gives do I give to you.
Let not your hearts be troubled, neither let them be afraid."

JOHN 14:27 ESV

TRUTH FOR TODAY

God can replace my stress with His holy peace.

REFLECTION

If I'm really honest about my struggle with stress,
I'd have to say . . .

THERE IS *no fear in love,*

BUT PERFECT LOVE *casts out* FEAR.

I JOHN 4:18 ESV

ACTIVITY

When you're feeling stressed,
practice the 4 x 4 breathing exercise.

Breathe in-2-3-4

Hold-2-3-4

Release-2-3-4

Repeat-2-3-4

Rocky-Road Friendships

A little consideration, a little thought for others, makes all the difference.

EEYORE

Ugh. Robin hung up the phone, her stomach in knots. Pauline always overreacted to everything. At least, it felt that way to Robin.

Problem was, Pauline was an old friend. Their relationship dated back to high school. Yes, they were very different from each other, but Robin had always hoped they could remain close. However, the fact that Pauline always had to have her way was grating on Robin's nerves. And while Robin usually caved just to keep the peace, that peace wasn't long-lived. And she usually ended up feeling taken advantage of.

Rocky-road friendships are tough. There are some relationships that you really do need to walk away from. When you're dealing with manipulation, narcissism, or abuse of any kind, it's time to slam that door shut. Most relational issues, though, are just mild annoyances, not "see you never" situations.

Remember, friendships are meant to help us grow. Even difficult friendships can teach us important lessons. First Peter 4:8 encourages us to approach one another with love and compassion, covering each other's flaws rather than holding them against each other.

AFFIRMATION

They're not perfect, but I choose to love them anyway.

If you are trying to decide whether to walk away from a friendship or to lean in with love and compassion, take some time to talk to God about it. Remember, He is not a God of confusion, fear, anger, or anxiety. He is a God of love, peace, power, and hope. When making your decision on how to move forward in this friendship, ask yourself what sets well in your soul? And then take the next necessary steps, knowing He is by your side.

GOD SAYS

A friend loves at all times,
and a brother is born for a time of adversity.

PROVERBS 17:17 NIV

TRUTH FOR TODAY

Not all friendships are easy,
but true friends are worth fighting for.

REFLECTION

Sometimes I find myself in difficult relationships
and wish things were easier. Then God reminds me . . .

"TREAT PEOPLE *the same way* YOU WANT THEM TO TREAT YOU."

LUKE 6:31 NASB

ACTIVITY

Where does your friend fall on the following spectrum? Where do you fall? Place an X on the line closest to where your friend falls and an O where you do.

DEMANDING ———————————————— **EASY**

UNKIND ———————————————— **KIND**

UNGODLY ———————————————— **GODLY**

TAKING ———————————————— **GIVING**

IMPATIENT ———————————————— **PATIENT**

MONOPOLIZING ———————————————— **LISTENING**

JUDGEMENTAL ———————————————— **LOVING**

CLOSED ———————————————— **OPEN**

The Mirror Has Two Faces

The LORD doesn't see things the way you see them.
People judge by outward appearance, but the LORD looks at the heart.

I SAMUEL 16:7 NLT

When you look in the mirror, who do you see? Not what, but who. Do you see the woman everyone else sees, or have you created a different persona in your mind, a woman whom others could never love because of how she looks?

If so, you are definitely not alone. It's not unusual for gals of every shape, size, and color to beat themselves up over how they look, especially in the days of carefully angled, filtered photographs floating across social media. Most women see their beautiful friends and then hyperfocus on their own outward appearance, wishing they could change the bumps, wrinkles, and flaws.

If only they could, then others would find them acceptable. Lovable.

Take Lisa. After weeks of dieting, she'd only lost three pounds. With over thirty pounds left to lose, she still had a long way to go. It hardly seemed fair. Her husband could eat anything and never gain a pound, but if Lisa even looked at a candy bar, she put on weight.

Not that her husband seemed to notice or care that she was a little fluffier than when he'd married her. But she did. And whenever she was forced to look at her reflection in the mirror, Lisa grumbled and complained all over again.

AFFIRMATION

Today I refuse to let the mirror define me.

Maybe you can relate. You're not a fan of how you look. For those who struggle with insecurities like weight or other physical attributes they wish they could change, coming to grips with their unfiltered reflection can be tough!

Oh, but God loves you just the way you are! He's not a beauty contest judge! He's not scoring you less because of your physical appearance. He couldn't care less about your freckles, wrinkles, or warts. Those things don't matter to Him. He takes one look at you and says, "Hello there, my beautiful daughter!"

GOD SAYS

*Then God said, "Let us make mankind in Our image,
in Our likeness, so that they may rule over the fish in the sea
and the birds in the sky, over the livestock and all the wild animals,
and over all the creatures that move along the ground."*

GENESIS 1:26 NIV

TRUTH FOR TODAY

I am created in the image of God
and bear His likeness.

REFLECTION

Whenever I start feeling down
about the reflection in the mirror,
I should remember . . .

THE LORD *doesn't see things*

THE WAY YOU SEE THEM.

PEOPLE JUDGE BY *outward appearance,*

BUT THE LORD *looks at the heart.*

I SAMUEL 16:7 NLT

ACTIVITY

Study your face in the mirror
and write down your observations.

Corrosion

There are a hundred paths through the world that are easier than loving. But who wants easier?

MARY OLIVER

McKinsey decorated one of the walls in her home's foyer with crosses in a variety of sizes and styles. Every time she walked by the wall, she stopped and gave them a closer look. She remembered where every single one came from. Some—like the big wrought-iron one—were heavier than others. The little silver one was light in comparison.

Sometimes we may feel like we have a lot of crosses to bear. Our lives are like that wall—filled with the heavy weights and the not-so-heavy ones that seem to add up.

That elderly parent we have to take care of? That's one cross. That moody husband who never wants to do anything fun? That's another cross. That kiddo who won't do anything you tell him to do? That one seems huge. But the great big one—the wrought-iron cross that troubles you daily—if you're like McKinsey, you don't always talk about that one openly because the weight is just too much to bear.

AFFIRMATION

I will give my crosses to the Savior, for He alone can carry them.

McKinsey's marriage was in trouble, but no one knew. She and her husband did a terrific job of hiding their problems so that no one on the outside could tell. Their friends at church? Clueless. Her coworkers? They would be shocked to hear it. They heard McKinsey carry on about the kids, the latest vacation, her new home décor, and so on. They never heard about her husband's recent affair or his desire to leave for good.

Only when he chose to leave permanently was she forced to deal with that cross out in the open (nothing like having to come clean in a public way). Doing so required opening up, talking to a counselor and a team of close friends who prayed her through it. With their help, McKinsey was finally able to hand that cross off to the only One capable of carrying it—the One who died upon the cross to save her.

GOD SAYS

"Come to Me, all you who are weary and burdened,
and I will give you rest. Take My yoke upon you and learn from Me,
for I am gentle and humble in heart, and you will find rest for your souls.
For My yoke is easy and My burden is light."

MATTHEW 11:28–30 NIV

TRUTH FOR TODAY

Jesus wants to carry those weights
I've been lugging around.

REFLECTION

Sometimes I get loaded down
with the cares of this life and forget . . .

"WHOEVER WANTS

TO BE MY DISCIPLE

MUST *deny themselves*

AND *take up their cross daily*

AND *follow Me.*"

LUKE 9:23 NIV

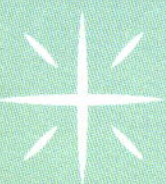

ACTIVITY

Here are some boulders I can get rid of today.
Fill in the blanks with weights you can lay down.

Beware the Pity Party

Fear makes the wolf bigger than he is.

GERMAN PROVERB

Bridget knew how to throw a terrific pity party, complete with food and beverages. She would drown her sorrows in chips, donuts, and cocoa and then wonder why she felt miserable the next day.

Sometimes her parties would go on longer than expected. When loneliness set in, for example. When she felt overlooked by her husband, her kids, or her friends. When the boss demanded too much of her. When financial woes caused too big a sting. Anytime the wolf howled at her door, she responded by barring herself inside and going into pity-party mode.

Maybe you know what it's like to throw a pity party. You pull out the streamers, reach for the sugary treats, and indulge while offering this common excuse: "I deserve it after all I've been through!"

Maybe it's time to ask God for a new plan of action. Remember, the wolf is rarely as big as he sounds when he's howling at the door. And also remember, he rarely gets through the door. Many of the things you're fretting over won't actually come to pass (whew!). So instead of throwing yourself into a frenzy and barring the door, you can invite a friend over for coffee, take a walk, or spend a little quiet time with God.

AFFIRMATION

I will not hand the leash of my life over to a big, bad wolf.

A little time to feel the weight of things is okay (in fact, sometimes it's downright needed), but it's always nice to think through ways to do it that leave you stronger and better off. Remember, God cares about your troubles, and the wolf has no power when you give the weight to the One who can hold it.

What are some ways you could draw near to God when you're tempted to wallow in self-pity? You never know, doing the last thing you feel like doing just might bring you some fresh reminders that your God is a God of comfort!

GOD SAYS

I was pushed back and about to fall,
but the LORD helped me.

PSALM 118:13 NIV

TRUTH FOR TODAY

Instead of giving in to wallowing in self-pity,
I can choose to draw closer to the God of comfort.

REFLECTION

When I start to feel sorry for myself,
I can always . . .

HE MAKES ME LIE DOWN IN *green pastures.*

HE LEADS ME BESIDE *still waters.*

HE *restores my soul.*

HE LEADS ME IN PATHS OF *righteousness*

FOR HIS NAME'S SAKE.

PSALM 23:2–3 ESV

ACTIVITY

Design an invitation to your very own pity party!

You are cordially invited to attend my pity party!

I AM FEELING SORRY FOR MYSELF BECAUSE

____

WHEN I'M FEELING DOWN-IN-THE-DUMPS, I ALWAYS EAT LOTS OF

____

WHEN YOU ARRIVE, PLEASE BRING

____

WE WILL LISTEN TO THE FOLLOWING SAD SONGS ON THE RADIO

____

AND I WILL WHINE ABOUT

____

THEN YOU WILL REMIND ME THAT THE BIBLE SAYS

____

AND THAT GOD WILL

____

Temper, Temper!

All of us fail, but this doesn't mean that we are failures.

ROBERT McGEE

Have you ever lost it? Like, really, really lost it? Maybe your toddler knocked over a bowl of spaghetti onto your freshly mopped floor and you hollered at him. Or perhaps you'd had enough with your boss's pushiness and you finally pushed back, but your words were laced with anger. It happens.

Some people seem to struggle more with anger than others. In fact, some make it a lifestyle . . . and they don't even seem to notice they're angry.

Such was the case with Brooke. She was grumpy most of the time. People at church noticed. People at her job noticed. And the kids? Well, there was no hiding it from them. They weren't exactly scared of her, but they were very aware of her volatile temper. She could turn on a dime and ruin everyone's day.

AFFIRMATION

I will do my best to make the necessary changes to live life with hope and joy.

Brooke's husband, Charlie, wasn't sure how to handle it without making the situation worse. When things reached the point where he just couldn't go on wondering all the time when the ever-bubbling volcano would erupt, Charlie reached out to someone on staff at church. Brooke agreed to counseling, which surprised him.

Turned out, she wanted to see change in her life as much as he hoped to see it. And when the counselor—a trusted friend—said, "Brooke, you are pretty grumpy most of the time," she saw the truth. If others were noticing, no doubt she really was a grump.

Maybe you're grumpy too. Maybe you live on the edge of irritability all the time, but you don't know how to get past it. Often irritability is rooted in discontentment—sadness that your life hasn't turned out as you'd hoped. Perhaps it's time to acknowledge that before God and allow Him to bring healing. When you let go of the frustrations and discontentment of yesterday, you can function better today and look forward to a brighter tomorrow.

GOD SAYS

Know this, my beloved brothers:
let every person be quick to hear,
slow to speak, slow to anger;
for the anger of man does not
produce the righteousness of God.

JAMES 1:19–20 ESV

TRUTH FOR TODAY

Give your anger to God before
things reach the boiling point.

REFLECTION

Lord, I feel like a volcano about to erupt at times,
but I'm so grateful You help me
get to the core of what's happening.
Here's what I'm really struggling with . . .

LET ALL BITTERNESS
AND WRATH AND ANGER AND
CLAMOR AND SLANDER
BE *put away from you,*
ALONG WITH ALL MALICE.

EPHESIANS 4:31 ESV

ACTIVITY

Before you reach the boiling point, write down the details of your anger.

WHAT'S ABOUT TO SPILL OVER?

WHO'S GOING TO GET HURT?

WHAT'S AT THE CORE OF YOUR VOLCANO?

WHAT WILL YOU DO TO COOL IT DOWN?

A Brave New Ending

Cure sometimes, treat often, comfort always.

HIPPOCRATES

Annie sat in the chair next to her best friend as Kay received the dreadful news: pancreatic cancer. Stage four.

The next few minutes—and hours—were a blur. Annie let Kay lead the way in the conversation that followed the doctor's visit. And, as they drove home, Annie tried to think of the right things to say, but nothing helpful came to her. How could she comfort her best friend after news like that?

Turned out, Kay did lead the way, in more ways than Annie could have imagined. In spite of not feeling well, Kay spent the next few weeks enjoying life to the fullest. She took her granddaughter on a kayak ride at a nearby lake. She celebrated her birthday at a pizza joint with a large group of wild friends. She settled her financial matters so the family wouldn't be burdened. And even as the situation grew more painful, she kept everyone entertained with her antics while hospitalized.

AFFIRMATION

No matter what I face, I can live with courage and joy, blessing those I love.

Every single day she kept Jesus front and center. Although her condition brought discomfort, she never complained. She was intentional about letting those she loved know how important they were to her. And right till the end, she never lost her patience with the hospital staff when she had to be monitored. She even saw her time with the nurses as an opportunity to share her faith with them.

Kay ended her journey on this earth with these words on her lips: "I can't wait to see Jesus." She died, just as she had lived, with a passion for her Savior and a heart filled with love.

Maybe you've had a friend like Kay. Her bravery astounded you. We have so much to learn from those who teach us how to have brave endings. Oh, how wonderful to live among friends who love Jesus and point us to Him, even in the hardest of situations!

GOD SAYS

Better is the end of a thing than its beginning,
and the patient in spirit
is better than the proud in spirit.

ECCLESIASTES 7:8 ESV

TRUTH FOR TODAY

I can still finish well if I have patience.

REFLECTION

Things are off to a rocky start,
but I can take control today by . . .

Join together IN FOLLOWING MY EXAMPLE,

BROTHERS AND SISTERS, AND JUST AS YOU HAVE

US AS A MODEL, *keep your eyes*

ON THOSE WHO LIVE AS WE DO.

PHILIPPIANS 3:17 NIV

ACTIVITY

Rewrite the ending of one of these popular fairy tales to show how a life story can change.

CINDERELLA'S FAIRY GODMOTHER NEVER SHOWS UP, BUT . . .

SLEEPING BEAUTY DOESN'T GET HER PRINCE CHARMING. INSTEAD . . .

. . . AND THEY LIVED HAPPILY EVER AFTER!

Ugh!

We must accept finite disappointment, but never lose infinite hope.

MARTIN LUTHER KING JR.

Corinne had a plan for how everything would work out. She would pick up her daughter from the airport at 7:45, swing back home to pick up her husband and the other kids, and then, together, they would all head out to her daughter's favorite restaurant for a late birthday dinner. If she had planned everything right, they would have just enough time for a quick meal before the restaurant closed.

But then evening traffic made her late to the airport. And when she got there, Corinne learned her daughter's flight had been delayed. Ugh! Half an hour later, she was still waiting.

Her beautiful daughter—the birthday girl—emerged exactly forty-seven minutes later than expected, all smiles. She had no idea about the planning that had gone into making her birthday special. She was just glad to be home from college to spend time with the family.

A short while later, the whole family sat in a fast-food joint that happened to be open late. Corinne felt like crying because things had gone so far south, but that sweet, oblivious daughter of hers didn't seem to notice or care.

She and her siblings were having one laugh after another as she shared funny antics of things that had happened back at school.

AFFIRMATION

My hope is in the Lord, not my circumstances.

Corinne finally relaxed when she realized that God had taken the situation and turned it around in His own special way.

Don't you love that difference in perspective? When we face those "Ugh!" moments, we can either get wound up or we can relax and enjoy the ride. The very moments we find frustrating often turn out to be memory-makers. So don't fret when things don't work out the way you planned. Likely, God's got something bigger and better in mind!

GOD SAYS

"So don't worry, because I am with you.
Don't be afraid, because I am your God.
I will make you strong and will help you;
I will support you with My right hand that saves you."

ISAIAH 41:10 NCV

TRUTH FOR TODAY

An "Ugh" day is not a "Give Up" day.

REFLECTION

I can turn my "ugh" around by . . .

"FOR *My thoughts are not your thoughts,*

NEITHER ARE YOUR WAYS MY WAYS,"

DECLARES THE LORD.

"AS THE HEAVENS ARE *higher than the earth,*

so are My ways HIGHER THAN YOUR WAYS

AND *My thoughts*

THAN YOUR THOUGHTS."

ISAIAH 55:8–9 NIV

ACTIVITY

Turn your "ugh" into a better word.
Write down as many words with "ugh"
in them as you can.

To the Fullest

The adventure of the Christian life begins when we dare to do what we would never tackle without Christ.

WILLIAM PENN

"What would Steven want you to do?" Paula asked.

Gillian looked at her friend. "What do you mean?"

"I mean . . ." Paula gave her a pensive look. "Steven was adventurous. Fun. And together, you were a force to be reckoned with, always off on some adventure or another. Now that he's gone . . ."

Her words drifted off, and Gillian sighed. "Now that he's gone, I'm not the same? Is that what you mean?"

"It's to be expected. You're grieving." Paula gave Gillian's hand a squeeze. "But I think Steven would want you to go on with those little adventures you used to have. Those road trips. The cruises. The big family theme parties."

AFFIRMATION

I am whole, not half.

"By myself?"

"No." Paula grinned. "With me. I'll be adventurous with you. I think it sounds like fun. Well, as long as you don't make me jump out of a plane or bungee jump or anything like that."

Gillian laughed at the image that presented.

"That's the first time I've heard you laugh in ages." Paula's lips tipped up in a smile. "So, what do you say? Are you in? Want to be adventure buddies? Because I, for one, think it sounds like a blast!"

Gillian thought about it for a second before nodding. "I'm in," she said at last. "You're right. Steven would want me to go on living."

"Not just living, but truly living every single moment to the fullest." Paula offered an encouraging nod. "That's how he was, and that's how you're meant to be."

Maybe you find yourself in Gillian's story. You've lost someone, and you wonder if all the adventure has gone out of your story. You think your best days are behind you. Half the journey is in deciding your best days are are yet to come. So begin to look at tomorrow as a bright, adventurous place, filled with possibility and wonder.

GOD SAYS

I commend joy, for man has nothing better under the sun
but to eat and drink and be joyful,
for this will go with him in his toil through the days of his life
that God has given him under the sun.

ECCLESIASTES 8:15 ESV

TRUTH FOR TODAY

When I start to fully enjoy life,
the adventure is just beginning.

REFLECTION

Joy transforms life into an adventure by . . .

In Him YOU HAVE BEEN *made complete.*

COLOSSIANS 2:10 NASB

ACTIVITY

Instead of fretting over all of
the dreams that haven't come true,
why not find joy for adventures to come?
Make a bucket list that is full of joy!

Empty Suitcases

God doesn't need a lot to do a lot. All David had was five stones. And all David used was one.

TONY EVANS

When Mary was a little girl, she dreamed of owning a record player. One Christmas when she was five years old, she opened a beautifully wrapped present that appeared to be her dream gift. Sure enough! The case was just the right size. It had to be!

Only, when she opened it, she discovered the case was empty inside.

A suitcase. Her parents had given her a little wooden suitcase. Didn't they realize the gift she really wanted? Hadn't she dropped enough clues?

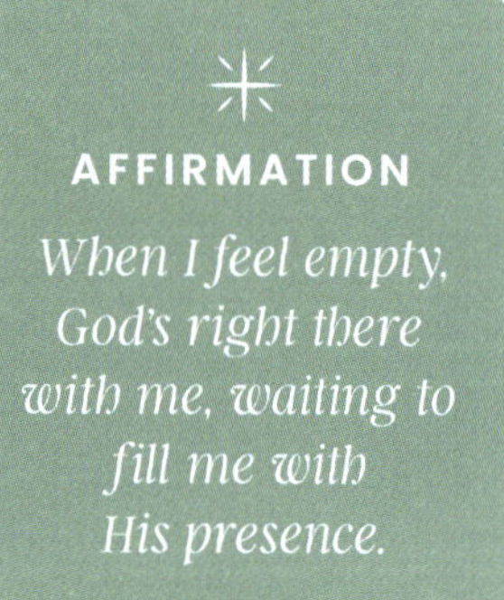

Mary was devastated, of course. But over time, that little suitcase became one of her favorite toys. She filled it with doll clothes. She used it to pack up her personal items when spending the night at her grandmother's house. She lugged all sorts of things around in it. And when she went off to college, she had to fight the temptation to take that little case with her. Instead, she packed it away in her parents' attic so that it would remain safe until she could pass it on to her own daughter someday.

That's how life is sometimes. We get our hopes up, and then they're dashed. We're as devastated as that five-year-old with the empty suitcase. Didn't we plant enough hints for God to figure out what we really wanted? Why would He let us down and give us something other than what we thought was best?

Here's a precious truth (learned only by experience): If we'll allow Him to, God will begin to show us the wonder of what's inside those so-called empty cases He places into our hands—all the things we didn't notice at first glance. And if we're really paying attention, we'll begin to see that what He's offering is far more valuable than anything we might have asked for ourselves.

He'll take the empty containers of our hearts and fill them in wondrous ways, if we let Him.

GOD SAYS

*From his fullness we have all received,
grace upon grace.*

JOHN 1:16 ESV

TRUTH FOR TODAY

Empty seasons feel like empty packages, but God is still there, pouring out blessings, even when we don't realize it.

REFLECTION

When I'm feeling empty or alone, one way God helps me feel less so is . . .

HE ALONE IS *my rock*

AND *my salvation,*

my fortress WHERE I WILL

NEVER BE SHAKEN.

PSALM 62:2 NLT

ACTIVITY

Think of a time when you did not receive the gift you wanted, when the package was empty. Then fill in the blanks to find what God intended.

I WAS EMPTY WHEN . . .

____

____

____

HOW GOD FILLED IT WITH UNEXPECTED BLESSINGS

____

____

____

I WAS EMPTY WHEN . . .

____

____

____

HOW GOD FILLED IT WITH UNEXPECTED BLESSINGS

____

____

____

Let's Rumble

I understand now that the vulnerability I've always felt is the greatest strength a person can have. You can't experience life without feeling life. What I've learned is that being vulnerable to someone you love is not a weakness. It's a strength.

ELISABETH SHUE

"I don't want to talk about it."

Ginger pushed the food around on her plate with her fork. Why did Aggie always feel the need to pry into things that weren't her business?

"Ginger, I just think it would help if you opened up about it." Aggie rested her hand on Ginger's, and Ginger realized her friend might not be prying. She might just want to help.

"You always push me away." Aggie's eyes misted. "And I get it. The stuff you're going through is hard to talk about. But please know that I'm right here when you're ready."

Ginger released a slow breath. Would this be the day she finally came clean and told someone about the depression she'd been walking through? Would Aggie—whose life seemed perfect in comparison—understand? Or would she judge her? Based on the compassion in her friend's eyes right now, she would understand.

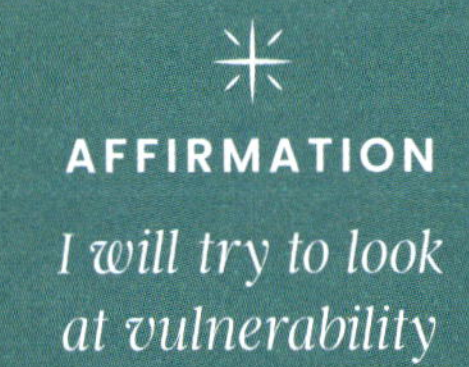

"Are you ready to get it all out? Because I'm here, if you are. And I've got all the time in the world," Aggie said.

After a moment's pause, Ginger began the difficult task of opening up. Finally. She made herself vulnerable to her best friend. Aggie listened and responded in love and offered to pray with her—right there in the restaurant. Why had she waited so long to open up?

Maybe you're like Ginger. You don't like to expose yourself to others for fear they won't get it. But the Bible encourages us to be honest in our friendships, without hiding our true selves. We are called to carry each other's burdens. And this requires being vulnerable enough to let others in, and then being open enough to receive their support.

GOD SAYS

Let your conversation be always full of grace, seasoned with salt, so that you may know how to answer everyone.

COLOSSIANS 4:6 NIV

TRUTH FOR TODAY

It's possible to be vulnerable, even if it requires a difficult (but necessary) conversation.

REFLECTION

When I have to have a hard conversation with someone, I usually start by . . .

"I AM WITH YOU; *that is all you need.*

My power SHOWS UP BEST IN WEAK PEOPLE."

NOW I AM GLAD TO BOAST

ABOUT *how weak I am*;

I AM GLAD TO BE A *living demonstration*

of Christ's power,

INSTEAD OF SHOWING OFF

MY OWN POWER AND ABILITIES.

II CORINTHIANS 12:9 TLB

ACTIVITY

Fill in the blanks.

The hardest conversation I ever had was with ______________________________

after he/she/I ____

____

____

____

It was one of those inevitable conversations that couldn't be avoided, but I felt

____

____

God used that day to change ______________________________________

____

____

I've learned that getting things out in the open is hard but ______________

____

____

Next time I have to have a difficult conversation with someone, I'll prepare first by

____

____

____

My Brain Is Broken

For I am a bear of very little brain,
and long words bother me.

WINNIE THE POOH

Ever had a day so off-kilter you felt like your brain was broken? Maybe you had so many items on your to-do list that the whole thing felt overwhelming, and you couldn't even figure out where to start.

Margaret had that problem. Her tiny town home was overrun with clutter. Each day the problem grew worse. She had no organizational system, so stuff went . . . well, everywhere.

One day, she finally decided she'd had enough. Today she would dive in.

Only, she couldn't figure out where to start. If she moved the items from the hall closet to the garage, then she would have to tackle the mess there to fit them in. And if she tackled the mess in the garage, then she would be forced to examine those boxes with all her deceased grandmother's personal items.

The more she thought about it, the muddier it all became in her mind. Maybe she should just wait until another day.

AFFIRMATION

When my heart is overwhelmed and my brain is feeling broken, I will lean on the Great Organizer!

No matter how big the mess is you've created in your personal space, there's a way out. Even if you're a clutter-bug and things are in a chaotic state, there are still brighter days ahead for you. Start with a list of all the things that need to be done, then spend some time praying over it. God will show you which items to tackle first. Remember that adage: "How do you eat an elephant? One bite at a time!" Tackle one or two items on your list every day. Or work on one room per day. Or one closet per day. The Lord will download a plan that makes sense to your schedule.

For sure, He has a better way for you than living in chaos. Your bright future includes a safe, healthy living environment, one that doesn't cause you distress. Before long, you'll be cozied up on the sofa with a cup of tea in hand, looking around at your beautiful, organized space.

GOD SAYS

Think about what I am saying, because the Lord will give you the ability to understand everything.

II TIMOTHY 2:7 NCV

TRUTH FOR TODAY

Even when I can't think clearly,
God can still give me the ability to understand.

REFLECTION

Sometimes when I get overwhelmed
and can't think straight, it helps me to . . .

WHEN *doubts* FILLED MY MIND,

YOUR *comfort* GAVE ME

renewed hope AND *cheer*.

PSALM 94:19 NLT

ACTIVITY

Write down the biggest task you're facing and make a plan.

THE BIG TASK IN FRONT OF ME

I'LL START BY

I CAN BREAK IT DOWN INTO CHUNKS LIKE

IN THE MEANTIME, I'LL KEEP MY FOCUS BY

The Valley So Low

I have been asked hundreds of times in my life why God allows tragedy and suffering. I have to confess that I really do not know the answer totally, even to my own satisfaction. I have to accept, by faith, that God is sovereign, and He is a God of love and mercy and compassion in the midst of suffering.

BILLY GRAHAM

Depression is more than a "low" feeling. It's more than a day or two of exhaustion on the sofa binge-watching your favorite TV series. True clinical depression can interrupt your life in a major way, affecting relationships, your family, your job, and even your ability to pay bills.

Robin wasn't sure what to call the season she was walking through. She had no "significant event" to blame it on. No relational breakup. No job loss or home foreclosure. Nothing big. But she just couldn't seem to pull herself up from the pit.

Her emotions were more volatile than usual, tears came more easily, and her energy level hit rock bottom. When a friend invited her out to lunch—something she would normally love to do—Robin just couldn't make herself go. She didn't have the energy. Instead, she nibbled on cookies and watched another pointless episode of a show she didn't even really like.

Maybe you've been there and you weren't sure how to lift yourself out of the doldrums. People said things like, "You have so much to be happy about" or "Your life is great! Why moan and groan?" but you couldn't seem to stop.

Check out this encouraging verse from Jeremiah 29:11 (ESV): "'For I know the plans I have for you,' declares the LORD, 'plans for welfare and not for evil, to give you a future and a hope.'" When you recognize that He's got big plans for all your tomorrows, it makes you want to do more than just trudge through today.

And remember, there's nothing shameful in admitting you need help. Reach out to a counselor, and if needed, visit a doctor for a checkup. God has big, bright things in store for you, and it's time to walk back out into the sunlight again.

AFFIRMATION

I will fight the temptation to dwell in the valley.

GOD SAYS

Even though I walk through the darkest valley,
I will fear no evil, for You are with me;
Your rod and Your staff, they comfort me.

PSALM 23:4 NIV

TRUTH FOR TODAY

I have nothing to fear in the "low" times
because God is right there, holding my hand.

REFLECTION

Instead of giving up when I'm suffering, I will . . .

"'FOR *I know the plans* I HAVE FOR YOU,'

DECLARES THE LORD,

'PLANS FOR *welfare and not for evil,*

TO GIVE YOU *a future* AND *a hope*.'"

JEREMIAH 29:11 ESV

ACTIVITY

Find the hidden words to discover actions you can take when you're in the valley.

S	B	H	M	I	Q	T	R	W	A	E	I	Z	H	P	E	C	O	K	R
N	R	J	G	G	S	O	T	F	O	N	Z	E	H	S	X	E	K	O	L
T	O	G	T	O	O	G	S	G	U	F	P	G	T	A	L	X	E	I	R
O	F	K	R	G	C	Y	T	O	K	E	E	A	O	E	E	R	C	O	L
R	S	X	D	I	R	F	E	D	A	S	R	T	R	J	C	D	B	R	L
D	D	N	A	P	P	R	J	D	T	Z	S	U	L	M	F	A	E	K	B
X	D	R	B	S	G	X	F	Z	D	U	I	E	G	B	R	B	L	A	G
E	C	I	N	P	F	L	U	P	R	N	S	T	Y	E	M	O	I	U	T
T	F	O	D	S	M	D	B	T	O	N	T	S	E	E	D	Y	E	L	A
H	S	A	V	O	F	V	D	H	U	O	T	R	M	N	W	A	V	M	S
T	T	A	O	G	X	S	W	O	H	E	T	E	S	C	S	T	E	H	N
O	F	C	I	O	L	C	C	P	N	F	R	A	I	O	C	E	B	I	T
R	I	O	N	T	P	D	U	E	A	T	E	D	V	U	O	A	B	B	X
I	N	Y	S	T	E	E	E	F	H	E	G	B	P	R	N	A	N	N	Y
A	E	A	O	V	S	T	E	N	V	E	E	I	O	A	T	Z	M	Z	J
E	G	D	T	E	I	V	H	K	G	Q	F	B	V	G	I	E	K	A	Y
O	M	R	G	H	I	K	R	A	A	H	N	L	D	E	N	V	I	A	I
P	H	O	L	S	P	S	O	K	C	F	T	E	A	D	U	W	R	E	T
R	S	H	N	R	S	I	V	Z	M	P	E	H	I	K	E	P	L	K	V
F	P	O	T	A	O	R	P	I	N	I	V	X	H	L	E	E	B	B	O

TRUST | BE ENCOURAGED | HOPE

CONTINUE | COUNSEL | REMEMBER

PRAY | READ BIBLE | BELIEVE

DON'T GIVE UP | PERSIST

True Selves

What we know matters, but who we are matters more.

BRENÉ BROWN

"Who are you?" If someone asked you that question, would you know how to answer?

You might say, "My name is so-and-so." Or maybe, "I'm Bobby and Cindy's mom."

You might respond with, "I'm a teacher" or "I work at a doctor's office."

If you're married, you might say, "I'm married to Joe."

But none of those things define you. Until you know who you really are—not what you do or whom you're related to—you will struggle to know your place in the world.

Before there was a husband or kids or a job, even before you drew your first breath, you were a child of the Most High God. And you're still His kid, even now. Once you realize Whose you are, you can know who you are.

When you come to fully understand what that means, when you have rooted and grounded your identity in Him, then your response to the "Who are you?" question will be made easier. You are a daughter of the King, fully loved and cared for. A plan has been in place for your life before you were ever even born—you are entirely unique, entirely special, entirely adored.

AFFIRMATION

Today I choose to recognize Whose I am so that I can fully understand who I am.

Knowing who you are will help you stick to your guns when you need to. But most of all, you'll have the assurance that the same God who created daffodils, cumulus clouds, crystal-blue Caribbean seas, and teensy-tiny tadpoles, created you as well. And He adores you with a love that goes beyond anything you could imagine.

This loving, gracious Creator has big things planned for you. The reason you can be assured of the fact that you have brighter days ahead is because He's the one illuminating them. And no one does a finer job of lighting your path than He does!

GOD SAYS

"God is spirit, and those who worship him must worship in spirit and truth."

JOHN 4:24 ESV

TRUTH FOR TODAY

I am not defined by my talents,
abilities, or physical appearance,
but by how deep my roots go down in Him.

REFLECTION

If someone were to ask, "Who are you . . . really?"
I would respond . . .

SEE HOW VERY MUCH *our Father loves us,*

FOR HE CALLS US *His children,*

AND THAT IS WHAT WE ARE!

BUT THE PEOPLE WHO *belong to this world*

DON'T RECOGNIZE THAT WE ARE GOD'S CHILDREN

BECAUSE *they don't know Him.*

I JOHN 3:1 NLT

ACTIVITY

Fill in the blanks below.

WHAT I LET OTHERS SEE (MY GIFTS, TALENTS, ACTIONS, LOOKS):

WHAT'S HIDING BENEATH THE SURFACE (MOTIVATIONS, INSECURITIES):

Shadows

It never hurts to keep looking for sunshine.

EEYORE

Scarlet curled up in her bed in the dark bedroom, listening to the wind howl outside. She could hear the sound of the sleet hitting the windows but could see nothing. The power had gone out thirty minutes ago. She prayed it would come back on soon, but with ice and snow covering the ground and the temperatures in the low teens, Scarlet wondered how—or if—she would see power anytime soon. It was well past midnight now. Others in the neighborhood were likely fast asleep, unaware of the darkness. But she couldn't rest her heart or mind.

How long could she keep her house warm in these conditions? And what about all the food in the refrigerator and freezer? She'd cooked soup in preparation for the cold snap. Would it all be wasted if the power didn't come back on? And how would she keep her two dogs warm?

After fretting for several minutes, Scarlet finally relaxed. God hadn't fallen off His throne. She had plenty of warm clothes and blankets. Her pups had sweaters. They could cuddle together in bed until the storm passed. And even if it lingered more than a few hours, her phone was charged. Her gas stove could still heat up soup once she used the lighter to get it going. Everything would end well, no matter how many hours—or even days—it took. She could trust God, even in the middle of the storm.

AFFIRMATION

I serve a God who can see in the dark.

Maybe you've been in a storm like that. You felt isolated. Alone. Discombobulated. But then you remembered, "Hey, God is still right here, doing what He always does—holding things together." Those endless nights, the ones that seem to go on forever? They really don't. The sun always breaks through in radiant splendor, and life goes on in glorious display. So hold on through the storm. The morning is coming.

GOD SAYS

The light shines in the darkness,
and the darkness has not overcome it.

JOHN 1:5 NIV

TRUTH FOR TODAY

Dark days will come,
but the light will break through every time!

REFLECTION

When dark clouds hover
and I get scared of what might be coming,
I try to remind myself . . .

Weeping MAY STAY FOR THE NIGHT,

BUT *rejoicing* COMES IN THE MORNING.

PSALM 30:5 NIV

ACTIVITY

Draw a line to connect the problem with the solution.

WHEN I AM AFRAID	Blessed is the man who remains steadfast under trial, for when he has stood the test he will recieve the crown of life, which God has promised to those who love him. JAMES 1:12 ESV
WHEN I FEEL ALONE	For God gave us a spirit not of fear but of power and love and self-control. II TIMOTHY 1:7 ESV
WHEN MY FAITH IS WEAK	And now, O Lord, for what do I wait? My hope is in you. PSALM 39:7 ESV
WHEN I NEED HOPE	"Have I not commanded you? Be strong and courageous. Do not be frightened, and do not be dismayed, for the LORD your God is with you wherever you go." JOSHUA 1:9 ESV
WHEN I FEEL LIKE GIVING UP	"If you have faith like a grain of mustard seed, you will say to this mountain, 'Move from here to there,' and it will move, and nothing will be impossible for you." MATTHEW 17:20 ESV

When Praying Seems Pointless

When God says no, we are sometimes tempted to wonder if He loves us. In reality, it's because He loves us, He sometimes says no.

LYSA TERKEURST

Have you ever been in a situation where prayer seemed pointless, where crying out to God felt like a futile endeavor? Maybe you've been through a crisis in the past and felt let down by His response . . . or what appeared to be His lack of response. Or maybe He answered no to a prayer and you got discouraged, so you decided to skip out on praying the next time.

Oh, sweet child of God! Prayer is a lifeline to your Creator, your one true link to the supernatural intervention of the only One who can help. Cutting Him out is the equivalent of cutting off your oxygen supply or shutting down the power to your house.

AFFIRMATION

I choose to believe that God hears my prayers and will answer in His time.

Don't cut that link, no matter how pointless praying might seem in the moment. If you could only see the things God is up to behind that invisible veil, you would be so excited! He's already putting plans in order, players in place, and hearts in motion. There's a heavenly chess game going on that you aren't able to see, but here's a fun fact: you're going to win this game.

You will. Even if things don't work out exactly as you might hope, you're going to come out stronger, healthier, more capable. And guess what else happens when you pray? It bolsters your confidence in the God of heaven and earth. Each day, as you stand in faith, you are growing into His own image. When that happens, you can believe for the impossible.

What seems impossible today? Have you stopped praying about it? Did you give up? Perhaps it's time to pick back up again so your precious heavenly Father can prove once again that your prayers—no matter how repetitive—are never pointless.

GOD SAYS

In the same way, the Spirit helps us in our weakness.
We do not know what we ought to pray for,
but the Spirit Himself intercedes for us
through wordless groans.

ROMANS 8:26 NIV

TRUTH FOR TODAY

My prayers might seem like nonsense at times,
but they are like oxygen to my soul,
keeping my hope alive.

REFLECTION

If giving up prayer is like giving up oxygen, then . . .

Rejoice ALWAYS, *pray* CONTINUALLY,

give thanks IN ALL CIRCUMSTANCES;

FOR THIS IS *God's will for you*

IN CHRIST JESUS.

I THESSALONIANS 5:16–18 NIV

ACTIVITY

If prayer is like oxygen, then how full is your tank today? Put a check mark next to the appropriate percentage.

O2

- [ ] 100%
- [ ] 75%
- [ ] 50%
- [ ] 25%
- [ ] 2%

If your tank is full, what steps can you take to maintain your connection to God?

___

___

___

___

If your tank is at the halfway point, what can you do to deepen your connection to God?

___

___

___

___

If your tank is running low, what steps can you take to restore your connection to God?

___

___

___

___

The Smallest of Moments

Keep your eyes on the stars
and your feet on the ground.
THEODORE ROOSEVELT

Cora was stuck at home, dealing with COVID symptoms. Living alone was tough enough during a regular, healthy season, but when facing something of this magnitude? She felt the aloneness more than ever. The first couple of days she wondered what it would be like to have someone close to take care of her.

Would she ever know that feeling?

After several rough days, she finally felt well enough to tend to some things around the house. While filling the dishwasher, she realized she'd neglected taking the trash to the curb . . . for over a week! And the can was loaded.

She waited until late at night, when everyone nearby would be sound asleep . . . just in case she was still contagious. Then she ventured outside to wheel the can to the curb. Clack, clack, clack . . . down the driveway she went with the noisy can, probably waking everyone in the neighborhood. Ugh.

As she came back up the driveway, Cora happened to glance up . . . and gasped. The night sky was brilliant, twinkling lights filling it in a wondrous show of God's handiwork. What she hadn't noticed with her hands full of trash, she now saw clearly.

AFFIRMATION

Today I will look for sparkling moments.

Cora paused and stared up, overcome by the beauty of it all. Off in the distance, a lovely moon hung low, a perfect orb of radiant light. It guided her back up the driveway and into the house once more.

Isn't that just how life is sometimes? You're down, feeling alone, doing the most mundane thing and then God shows up and shows off in the most marvelous way! You don't notice it at first because you're dealing with the icky stuff. But when you release those things into His hands, He proves to you that He was right there all along, even when you felt alone.

GOD SAYS

On the glorious splendor of your majesty,
and on your wondrous works, I will meditate.

PSALM 145:5 ESV

TRUTH FOR TODAY

A baby's smile, an ocean wave, a brilliant night sky . . .
God's beauty is all around me
if I will just take the time to look.

REFLECTION

When I fully experience God's magnificent creation,
I often feel . . .

WHATEVER IS *good and perfect*

IS A *gift* COMING DOWN TO US

FROM *God our Father,*

WHO CREATED ALL THE LIGHTS IN THE HEAVENS.

HE *never changes*

OR CASTS A SHIFTING SHADOW.

JAMES 1:17 NLT

ACTIVITY

Have you had "stargazing moments," times when you stopped to marvel at God's creation, large or small? List some of the special, breathtaking moments in your life that offered you glimpses of God's handiwork.

A Place to Belong

Friendship is born at the moment when one persons says to another "What! You too? I thought I was the only one."

C.S. LEWIS

Anita loved her foster dog, Gabriel. He was the cutest thing—a terrier mix with black and white fur and deep brown eyes. The sweet darling had been rescued off the streets. He was skinny and frail and completely unsocialized. No one knew how long he'd been wandering around out there, but Anita was so happy to have him with her now. He arrived at her home on December 18, just before Christmas, so she gave him the name Gabriel. He earned it with his stellar behavior.

Not long after Gabe's arrival, Anita got sick with the flu. She couldn't leave her house for several days, and the little dog provided just the right amount of company. He loved to snuggle, just what she needed. And he didn't require much care—just some food, water, and a few tummy tickles. At the end of her illness, Anita knew she couldn't let this special guy go. She would have to adopt him and make him her fur-ever pup.

AFFIRMATION

Great relationships are worth waiting for.

Maybe you feel a bit like Gabriel. You haven't really fit in anywhere, though not for lack of trying. You're like a pup wandering the streets, feeling like you don't have a place to belong. Those women at work, the ones who are always going out to lunch together? Why don't they invite you? Your two sisters? They seem so close to each other but not to you. That neighbor you've tried to connect with? Why is she always so busy?

Oh, but don't give up just yet! Like it was for Gabriel, the perfect fit is ahead. That sweet pup wasn't meant to walk alone, and neither are you. There will be friends, companions, confidants . . . all you could want and more. But you have to keep putting yourself out there to meet the perfect ones. When you do, it will be as cozy and comfortable as Gabriel and Anita, curled up on the sofa together.

GOD SAYS

"For where two or three are gathered in my name, there am I among them."

MATTHEW 18:20 ESV

TRUTH FOR TODAY

True fellowship with friends keeps Christ at the center.

REFLECTION

It's not always easy to find the perfect friend group, but I'm learning . . .

"I *no longer* CALL YOU *servants,*

BECAUSE A SERVANT

DOES NOT KNOW HIS MASTER'S BUSINESS.

INSTEAD, I HAVE CALLED YOU *friends,*

FOR EVERYTHING THAT I LEARNED FROM MY FATHER

I have made known to you."

JOHN 15:15 NIV

ACTIVITY

What places make you feel . . .

SOCIALLY CONFIDENT?

NERVOUS?

MELANCHOLY?

LIKE YOU FIT IN?

LOVED?

The Superhighway

When everything you've hoped and prayed for doesn't happen the way you thought it would, rest your weary heart and know that God is drawing you close to Him and He is not abandoning your dreams. He is holding your heart close to His.

KATY FULTS

Bridget loved the elephant ear plants that her husband put in the back garden. They were luscious and green and filled the space with beauty. When it rained, droplets formed on those big, vibrant leaves and glistened in the afternoon sunlight. More than anything, they reminded her of a trip she'd once taken to a tropical paradise.

Every winter they would die off, and her husband would trim them back. But then, in the spring, there they were again, in all their glory . . . bigger and more vibrant than ever. Those gorgeous plants took her breath away. They also energized her and made her want to work harder on the rest of her garden.

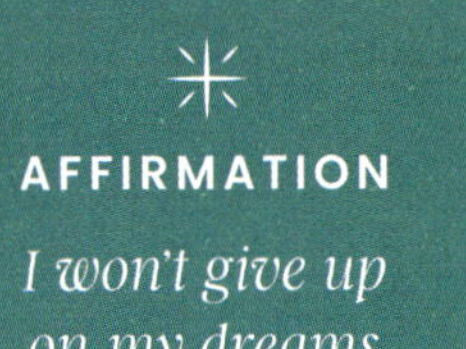

Maybe you've had dreams like that. They started off big and beautiful. Then an unexpected winter season came along and drove them into the ground. They died off, and you thought you would never see a resurrection season. After a while, you gave up.

Let's face it: Dreams don't always come true. People don't always catch the vision for the things you hope to accomplish. But that doesn't mean you should give up. Even during seasons when those elephant ears die off, there's the anticipation that they will return in the spring. When the warmth of the sun breaks through . . . *bam!* Spring! Suddenly the possibilities stretch out in front of you like a superhighway stretching into the great beyond.

God has plenty of springtimes ahead for you. This is just a wintry spell. That ice will melt, and when it does . . . look out! The superhighway will call your name!

GOD SAYS

A joyful heart is good medicine,
but a crushed spirit dries up the bones.

PROVERBS 17:22 ESV

TRUTH FOR TODAY

As I travel along life's bumpy highway,
the journey will be better if I choose joy.

REFLECTION

Not every day is a perfect day,
but even on bad days I can . . .

Delight yourself IN THE LORD,

AND HE WILL *give you*

THE *desires of your heart.*

PSALM 37:4 ESV

ACTIVITY

Want to get rid of the blues?
Ask God to help you design your perfect day.

PLACES TO GO

PEOPLE TO SEE

FOODS TO EAT

THINGS TO DO

PEOPLE TO BLESS

Let Down the Load

Don't underestimate the value of Doing Nothing,
of just going along,
listening to all the things you can't hear,
and not bothering.

A. A. MILNE

Fran dreamed of hiking in the Rocky Mountains. She talked her husband into a trip to nearby Estes Park, a lovely, scenic village. Their plan? To hike during the afternoon and enjoy the town in the evenings and mornings.

Their first day on the hiking trail, Fran found herself regretting her decision—not to hike, but to carry the backpack filled with so much stuff. They weren't really going that deep into the mountains, so why did she need so many provisions? Maybe she'd over-prepared, if such a thing was possible.

A careful reassessment took place once they returned to the hotel that evening. The next day she went with a smaller, lighter pack. It held only the things she might actually use, should an emergency arise. They kept to well-marked trails and didn't venture far out, just in case.

Fortunately, they didn't need any of their provisions except food and water. Well, she did need a bandage for a blister on her foot, but she happened to have one in her pack.

AFFIRMATION

Today I choose to step away from the chaos and just be.

Can you relate to Fran's trailblazer plight? Have you ever carried a heavy load? Uphill? In rough terrain? Maybe it's time to ask God to remove everything that is weighing you down. Cast off the weight that so easily besets you, hems you in, causing you to freeze in place. Hand that pack to Jesus and watch Him carry the load for you. Before long, you'll be breezing up the trail, leaving your worries in the dust.

GOD SAYS

"The thief's purpose is to steal and kill and destroy. My purpose is to give them a rich and satisfying life."

JOHN 10:10 NLT

TRUTH FOR TODAY

I can have a rich and satisfying life, no matter what I'm facing.

REFLECTION

When I think of the words *rich* and *satisfying*, I usually think . . .

LET HIM HAVE

ALL YOUR *worries* AND *cares*,

FOR HE IS ALWAYS *thinking about you*

AND WATCHING EVERYTHING

that concerns you.

I PETER 5:7 TLB

ACTIVITY

If your life were a newspaper headline,
what would it say right now?

Pocketbook Woes

My flesh and my heart may fail, but God is the strength of my heart and my portion forever.

PSALM 73:26 NIV

Whenever Lila would get stressed out over her finances, she would bake. Cookies. Cakes. Brownies. Pies. Didn't matter. Stress called for baking. There was something about being in the kitchen, creating something tasty and beautiful, that made everything better again.

Unwilling to eat all her baked goods, she started taking them to work to share with coworkers. Before long, they started asking for more.

"That chocolate cake you brought last Tuesday was the best I've ever eaten. Would you bake one for my husband's birthday next month? I'll pay you."

"Girl, I've never had cupcakes decorated as pretty as the ones you brought in for Valentine's Day. Could I get you to make some for my daughter's graduation? I'd rather give the money to you than the grocery store."

"Those oatmeal cookies were better than my grandmother's, but don't tell her I said so, okay? Could you bake a couple dozen for my book club?"

It didn't take long to see that God was providing a way past some of the financial woes, and He used her existing gift to do it. With the additional income from baking, she was able to get caught up on that credit card debt. And, once caught up, she kept right on baking and tucking money aside for a rainy day. She also had a blast learning more about the craft and furthering her skills.

AFFIRMATION

I won't allow my bank balance to rob me of my joy.

Lila would say that God turned lemons into lemonade. Or, in this case . . . lemon-blueberry cake. With a yummy glaze on top.

What has you stressed out today? Finances? Car troubles? Work problems? Remember, like Lila, the Lord already sees the solution, long before you do. Ask Him to download His plan, so that you can rest easy in His provision, even before you see it with your own eyes. And don't be surprised if He uses a gift He's already been stirring up.

GOD SAYS

The love of money is a root of all kinds of evils.
It is through this craving that some
have wandered away from the faith
and pierced themselves with many pangs.

I TIMOTHY 6:10 ESV

TRUTH FOR TODAY

God can help me turn
this financial situation around.

REFLECTION

If I were to describe my relationship with money,
I would say . . .

MY FLESH AND MY HEART *may fail,*

BUT GOD IS THE *strength* OF MY HEART

AND *my portion forever.*

PSALM 73:26 NIV

ACTIVITY

Using the prompts below, fill out a prescription for financial relief.

EXAMPLE

Rx name: Financial Relief Formula
Usage: Daily Administration of prayer and reflection.
Side Effects: Increased peace. Improved focus.
Expected Outcome: Confidence that God will meet your needs.

Rx NAME

____

____

____

USAGE

____

____

____

SIDE EFFECTS

____

____

____

EXPECTED OUTCOME

____

____

____

No Permanent Blots

We need to understand that failing can be a step toward maturity, not a permanent blot on our self esteem.

ROBERT McGEE

Jane let out a cry as she saw the black marks all over her brand-new French Provincial bedroom suite. She turned to discover her three-year-old daughter with a marker in hand.

Her clothing and face were also covered.

"Oh, Trisha! How could you?" Jane pulled the marker from her hand and rushed her to the bathroom to scrub the stains off.

Only, they wouldn't come off, no matter how hard she scrubbed. Neither would they come off her once-gorgeous white furniture. She did her best, but there was no removing those black marks.

It took days for Trisha to look normal; the furniture stayed marked even years after. It stood as a testament to her daughter's naughtiness (and Mom's punishment for getting too wrapped up in a phone call to notice).

Maybe you've experienced something like that. Maybe a beautiful dress was ruined because of one spill. Maybe a dress shirt got an ink stain in the pocket. Maybe the couch had a spot where the dog chewed through the fabric.

Hey, these things happen! But they really can wreck your day (or even your week or your year, depending on the cost of the destruction).

Those permanent blots are reminders of the bad thing that happened. Every time you see them, you relive the event all over again. Ugh! Sometimes the only way to get rid of the memories is to toss the item or (in the case of the furniture) to paint over the stains in the hopes that you can hide them.

Aren't you glad there are no permanent blots on your record? As soon as you asked Jesus to remove them, He did! He doesn't look at you and see black marks. No, when He looks at you, He sees French Provincial all the way.

Because God forgives and forgets, you can move forward with confidence and joy. There's nothing to hold you back. Your record is clean!

AFFIRMATION

It's never too late to begin again.

GOD SAYS

*If we confess our sins, He will forgive our sins,
because we can trust God to do what is right.
He will cleanse us from all the wrongs we have done.*

I JOHN 1:9 NCV

TRUTH FOR TODAY

I don't have to wonder if God has forgiven me.
If I ask, He forgives.

REFLECTION

In spite of God's forgiveness, sometimes I feel . . .

LET US GO RIGHT INTO *the presence of God*

WITH *sincere hearts* FULLY TRUSTING HIM.

FOR OUR GUILTY CONSCIENCES

HAVE BEEN SPRINKLED WITH CHRIST'S BLOOD

TO *make us clean*, AND OUR BODIES

HAVE BEEN WASHED WITH *pure water*.

HEBREWS 10:22 NLT

ACTIVITY

It's time to take inventory. Are there stains on your heart?
If so, admit them and ask God for His forgiveness.

Bullets

We are here to thrive.
Not to sometimes survive.

EZINNE ORJIAKO, NKEM.

There's always that one person. You know the one. She takes advantage of you at work. And then, after bad-mouthing and mistreating you, she takes the credit for all you've done.

It makes your stomach curdle, the way she brags about how she manages the best department on the team. You want to rat her out to the boss, but he's so busy he wouldn't really pay much attention. And what would he do about it, anyway? He just wants to get the job done and move on. Thanks to your hard work, the job is getting done, so he's a happy man. But you? You're exhausted.

You decide to keep quiet, but inside you're seething. You work harder than anyone else, but that doesn't stop this woman from harassing you, carrying on about how you need to improve. Her words are like bullets to the heart. And for what? So that her star can shine brighter? Hardly seems fair.

It's hard to know how to thrive in situations like this, but remember . . . you are where you are for a reason. And if it's the wrong reason—if you're really meant to be someplace else—God will show you. He will give you a way out. In the meantime, know that you've got a bright future and she can't rob you of that, so don't waste your thoughts on her antics. Just do the best job you can under the circumstances and grow in faith and experience. And if the right opportunity presents itself (pray about it!), you might find an open door to talk to your boss privately. Instead of walking in with a heart full of bullet holes, you'll be able to face him with strength and dignity.

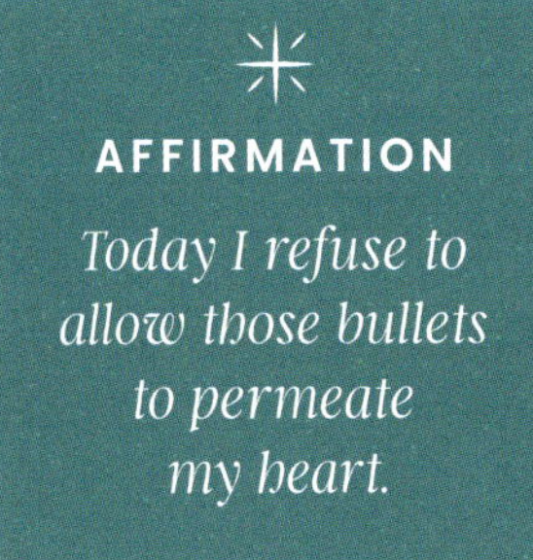

GOD SAYS

Don't make friends with quick-tempered people
or spend time with those who have bad tempers.
If you do, you will be like them.
Then you will be in real danger.

PROVERBS 22:24–25 NCV

TRUTH FOR TODAY

Difficult people are tough to deal with,
but God will give me wisdom
to walk away when necessary.

REFLECTION

When friendship drama rears its head, I usually . . .

NEVERTHELESS, EACH PERSON SHOULD LIVE

AS *a believer* IN WHATEVER SITUATION

THE LORD *has assigned to them,*

JUST AS GOD HAS CALLED THEM.

THIS IS THE RULE

I LAY DOWN IN *all the churches.*

I CORINTHIANS 7:17 NIV

ACTIVITY

Different people trigger different feelings. Complete the facial expressions to express how you feel when you're with difficult people.

PERSON'S INITIALS / NAME / CODE NAME

____

PERSON'S INITIALS / NAME / CODE NAME

____

PERSON'S INITIALS / NAME / CODE NAME

____

PERSON'S INITIALS / NAME / CODE NAME

____

Cracks in the Earth

To the brave and brokenhearted
who have taught us how to rise after we fall.
Your courage is contagious.

BRENÉ BROWN

Susan couldn't make any sense out of the things her sister was saying. The words were nonsensical, filled with bizarre details. And her sister's over-the-top animation troubled her almost as much. This wasn't the first time she'd heard Karen talk like this or get so wound up about things that made no sense to anyone else. From time to time, her younger sister would get extremely agitated and go off on a tangent in dramatic fashion. And it never made sense, any of it.

Sometimes things ended with Karen getting angry and threatening. Those incidents were frightening. Susan suspected mental illness but didn't know how to broach the subject. After one particularly frightening episode where her sister began throwing valuables away, Susan decided to approach Karen's husband to get his take on things.

Turned out, he was relieved someone else had noticed. Together they managed to talk Karen into going to a psychiatrist, where she was diagnosed with schizophrenia. After getting on some medication, things calmed down, but after a while they started up again. The next few years were like a pendulum, swinging back and forth. When Karen stayed on her meds, things weren't bad, but then she would think she was cured and would stop the medication altogether. Things would go off the rails again.

Maybe you're loving a family member or friend through a similar crisis. It's hard to know what to do when someone you love is struggling with mental illness. God never meant for us to walk this road alone. That's why you've got to have help. You need a team of trusted people who know what they're doing. This is one road you were never meant to walk alone.

AFFIRMATION

The cracks are deep, but God's love is deeper still.

GOD SAYS

Two are better than one,
because they have a good reward for their toil.
For if they fall, one will lift up his fellow.
But woe to him who is alone when he falls
and has not another to lift him up!

ECCLESIASTES 4:9–10 ESV

TRUTH FOR TODAY

Friendships are not without their challenges,
but two are better than one.
God created me to live in community.

REFLECTION

When I think about the friends
God has surrounded me with, I . . .

GOD IS OUR *refuge* AND *strength*,

A VERY *ready help* IN TROUBLE.

PSALM 46:1 NASB

ACTIVITY

Friendships are like . . .

CLEANING THE TOILET BECAUSE

PLAYING CARDS BECAUSE

BAKING A CAKE BECAUSE

CLIMBING A MOUNTAIN BECAUSE

DRINKING A HOT BEVERAGE BECAUSE

DUSTING THE FURNITURE BECAUSE

RUNNING A MARATHON BECAUSE

EATING ICE CREAM BECAUSE

The Picture of Perfection

No relationship is all sunshine,
but two people can share one umbrella
and survive the storm together.

UNKNOWN

Have you ever felt like you didn't fit in with the church crowd? Sometimes those folks can be a little too, well . . . perfect. Or so they seem. You don't hear them saying the wrong thing or doing the wrong thing. Their kids aren't in trouble at school or facing down a police officer for damaging someone else's property. No, their kiddos are on the honor roll or volunteering in the nursery at church. Their husbands? Leading the men's Bible study, of course.

Where did you go wrong? How come you didn't get the perfect Christian life like she did? You've done your best, after all. But you can barely find time to cook a meal for yourself, let alone deliver one to a sick family. And when you quote a Bible verse, it's usually something like, "Vengeance is mine; I will repay, saith the Lord" (Romans 12:19 KJV). You've got that one memorized. You want to volunteer at church, but who has time for all that? You're not getting enough sleep as it is.

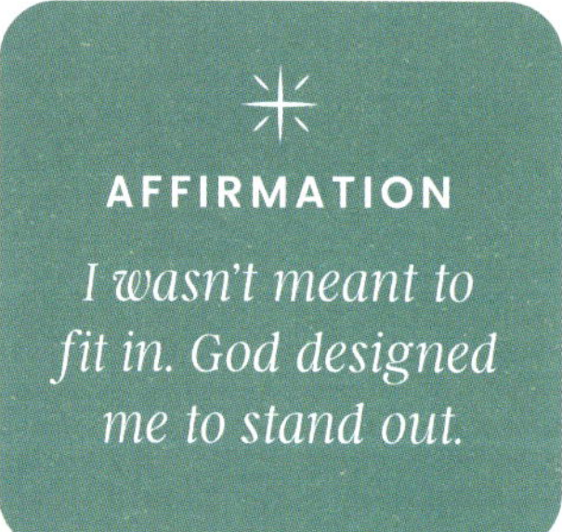

Now, the goal's not to let excuses keep you from doing good things, and sure, maybe she is practically perfect in every way. But you know what? External appearances (especially a churchy façade) can be deceiving. More likely she's far from the picture of perfection you've painted in your head.

But even if she really is as amazing as she seems, so are you! God is using you to bring a smile to others and to lift their spirits with your crazy antics. They may not be as glamorous, but you have your own ways of serving. Besides, not everyone is made to fit in. So don't work so hard to be like everyone else. Let them get to know you just as you are—the flawed, imperfect, wonderful you.

GOD SAYS

Each one should test their own actions.
Then they can take pride in themselves alone,
without comparing themselves to someone else,
for each one should carry their own load.

GALATIANS 6:4–5 NIV

TRUTH FOR TODAY

They might seem practically perfect in every way,
but no one is perfect except God.

REFLECTION

When I'm tempted to compare myself
to other, "better" Christians, I should remind myself . . .

IT IS *God Himself*

WHO HAS MADE US WHAT WE ARE

AND GIVEN US *new lives*

FROM CHRIST JESUS.

EPHESIANS 2:10 TLB

ACTIVITY

Instead of cutting yourself down or comparing yourself to others, why not take note of some of the accomplishments you've made over the years? God is proud of you, for being you!

SOMETHING I GOT RIGHT

___

___

___

SOMETHING I GOT RIGHT

___

___

___

SOMETHING I GOT RIGHT

___

___

___

SOMETHING I GOT RIGHT

___

___

___

No Sugarcoating

*Instead, we will speak the truth in love,
growing in every way more and more like Christ,
who is the head of His body, the church.*

EPHESIANS 4:15 NLT

Mirabelle paced the room and tried to think of a way to share the story with her husband. He needed to know that their son had been expelled from school for getting into a fight with another boy. But Robert wouldn't take it well. They'd been through this sort of thing before. Multiple times, in fact.

Still, there was no sugarcoating the story. She couldn't very well unsuspend her son now, could she? Robert would have to know, and she had to be the one to tell him.

Maybe you've been in a rough situation like that, where you had to share not-so-great news with someone you loved. You couldn't think of a way to transition with ease into the subject, so you just blurted it out.

Usually getting the truth out there is better than beating around the bush, anyway. Whether it's telling your husband about that big purchase you put on the credit card or admitting to your boss that you made a huge accounting error during the last billing cycle—getting things over with is always best.

And while you're at it, it's time to have that "hard talk" with your son, as well. You know the one. Instead of dancing around his issues, you've got to speak the truth in love so that he grows up into a healthy, stable man, not one who pushes others around.

Is it easy to speak hard truths? No. And you might be quivering as you think about how hard it might be. But it's always worth it. Friendships can be saved. Marriages can be healed. Work relationships can be restored. Children's lives can be changed. Addicted friends can be set free.

All this and more . . . when you speak the truth in love.

AFFIRMATION

It's not going to be easy, but I will do my best to speak the truth in love, then watch for a miracle!

GOD SAYS

Do not let any unwholesome talk come out of your mouths,
but only what is helpful for building others up
according to their needs,
that it may benefit those who listen.

EPHESIANS 4:29 NIV

TRUTH FOR TODAY

It makes God's heart happy when I guard my mouth
and only speak kind, loving words to others.

REFLECTION

If I'm really being honest, I have to say that
the things that come out of my mouth are sometimes . . .

INSTEAD, WE WILL SPEAK
THE TRUTH *in love,*
GROWING IN EVERY WAY
MORE AND MORE *like Christ,*
WHO IS THE *head of His body,*
THE CHURCH.

EPHESIANS 4:15 NLT

ACTIVITY

Think of something you recently said in anger or frustration. Write it down. Then think of a better way to say what needed to be said.

WHAT I SAID

A BETTER WAY TO SAY IT

Turn, Turn, Turn

Circumstances are the rulers of the weak; they are but the instruments of the wise.

SAMUEL LOVER

If you learned anything from the COVID-19 season, it's this: nothing is predictable. Everything is subject to change, often without notice. You can make all the plans you like, but in the blink of an eye, everything can shift. Precious opportunities might slip through your fingers.

That trip you had planned? Looks like it's off. That family holiday you had hoped to host? Not happening. Your daughter's much-anticipated graduation from high school? Ugh. That one really hurt.

So how do you handle it when the unexpected things happen? When you're faced with a sudden financial woe or an unwanted health crisis? How do you manage when your plans for a vacation are thwarted or a job opportunity slips through your fingers? Change isn't easy. It takes a lot of energy to stop something you're doing, completely rethink your plan, and go a different way. But you can do it! You're learning from these disappointments. A lot.

AFFIRMATION

Today I refuse to stress myself out about things I cannot control or change.

Did you learn some lessons from 2020, perhaps? Part of what makes life so adventurous is not knowing how things will turn out. But if you're a control freak, not knowing what is around the corner can be scary. Maybe it's time to learn how to "let go and let God." The year 2020 might have looked like letdown after letdown, but even those who've been the most disappointed still have a bright future.

Things happen. Life happens. Unavoidable circumstances happen. But you can't allow those things to control how you feel about your future. It's just as bright as it ever was (copper penny bright, in fact). So don't give in to those feelings of hopelessness. They are, after all, just feelings.

Will you allow God to take the mess and turn it into a hopeful message for the days ahead?

GOD SAYS

Your eyes saw my unformed body;
all the days ordained for me
were written in Your book
before one of them came to be.

PSALM 139:16 NIV

TRUTH FOR TODAY

My life is a beautiful script,
fully written, directed, and orchestrated
by the Creator of all, who knows me best
and loves me most.

REFLECTION

When life is unpredictable, I'll just yell "Plot Twist!"
and remember that God . . .

THE LORD HIMSELF *goes before you*

AND WILL *be with you;*

HE WILL NEVER LEAVE YOU

NOR FORSAKE YOU.

DO NOT BE *afraid;*

DO NOT BE *discouraged.*

DEUTERONOMY 31:8 NIV

ACTIVITY

What would the script of your life look like?

THE BACKSTORY ______________________________

____

____

THE TURNING POINT ______________________________

____

____

NEW CHANCES ______________________________

____

____

PLOT TWIST! ______________________________

____

____

SETBACK ______________________________

____

____

FINAL PUSH ______________________________

____

____

HOPEFUL ENDINGS ______________________________

____

____

This Is a Test

The truth of the matter is, this too will pass, and we'll get through it with more peace and stability if we'll trust God to do what is best for us at the right time and in His way.

JOYCE MEYER

Pop quizzes weren't Linda's thing. Once, in Bible college, she found herself facing a pop quiz in her Old Testament survey class. Who were King David's sons? She had no idea.

In a moment of what she thought was sheer brilliance, she penciled in "Larry, Moe, and Curly."

Unfortunately, her professor didn't find her answers as funny as she did. She got a very low score on the pop quiz.

AFFIRMATION

With God's help, I can ace this test.

As much as we try to avoid them, life is filled with pop quizzes. There are relational tests, faith tests, even financial tests. And though you often come out of them feeling like a failure, there's no "pass or fail" with God. He's simply hoping you learn and grow from the testing seasons you walk through.

Courtney did. She and her husband went through a rough patch when they lost their home to foreclosure. Zach became ill and lost his job. They fell behind on the mortgage, and—even after he recovered from his illness—they couldn't get caught back up.

In the throes of it, Courtney did her best not to panic. She sent letters and emails to the mortgage company, offering to work things out, but they did not respond as she'd hoped.

God opened a door for a rental home that was considerably larger than the house they were losing, so the family made the move, and their original home went back to the bank. It left a horrible stain on their credit that took years to clear off, but Courtney and her husband went on to buy that rental and make it their own.

A test can (and usually does) become a testimony, if you keep trusting God through it. He hasn't brought you this far to leave you hanging now! He's got big things ahead for you!

GOD SAYS

The LORD *your God is testing you*
to find out whether you love Him
with all your heart and with all your soul.

DEUTERONOMY 13:3 NIV

TRUTH FOR TODAY

Because I love God with my whole heart,
I will pass safely through the tests
that come my way.

REFLECTION

I will confess, I haven't passed
all of God's tests immediately.
Sometimes I react poorly and . . .

Examine yourselves TO SEE

WHETHER YOU ARE IN THE FAITH;

test yourselves.

DO YOU NOT REALIZE THAT

Christ Jesus is in you—

UNLESS, OF COURSE,

YOU FAIL THE TEST?

II CORINTHIANS 13:5 NIV

ACTIVITY

Write down a few of life's recent "tests" and grade yourself. How did you do on a pass/fail scale?

WHAT I WENT THROUGH:

PASS..FAIL

WHAT I WENT THROUGH:

PASS..FAIL

WHAT I WENT THROUGH:

PASS..FAIL

The Courage to Keep Standing

Courage is contagious. When a brave man takes a stand, the spines of others are often stiffened.

BILLY GRAHAM

Have you ever had a "chronic" issue? Maybe you had a nagging toothache that just wouldn't go away. Or perhaps you struggle with arthritis pain that can be considered "chronic" because it gives you grief on a daily basis.

Some people deal with autoimmune diseases—diabetes, rheumatoid arthritis, or lupus, to name a few. Others are fighting a battle against fibromyalgia or neurosensory issues. These folks have come to know the word *chronic*. They wish they didn't have ongoing health issues, but the struggle is real.

So what do you do if you're one of the millions in chronic pain? How do you cope? How does the desire to be pain-free affect your faith? Do you really stand a chance of things getting better?

AFFIRMATION

In this world I will have tribulation, but Jesus has overcome the world.

There's a wonderful story in the New Testament about a woman who struggled with a chronic illness. The gospel of Matthew calls her the woman "with an issue of blood" (9:20 KJV), which tells us that she had chronic hemorrhaging. When she heard Jesus was in town, she worked her way through the crowd until she could touch the hem of His garment. Healing immediately coursed through her body!

Jesus, feeling the healing power going forth, called out, "Who touched Me?" (Luke 8:45 KJV). Do you think He actually needed an answer? No, He already knew who had touched Him. He wanted her to speak it, to make it real. He knew it would increase her faith. It also immediately changed the village's perception of her. No longer "unclean," she would now be welcomed back in society.

He wants you to make it real too. Today, lean into Him. No matter how many times you've already prayed, pray again. Don't stop fighting. Whether your miracle comes through a divine touch (healing) or through a deeper relationship with Him through the pain, the safest place to be is touching Him.

GOD SAYS

Let us not grow weary of doing good,
for in due season we will reap,
if we do not give up.

GALATIANS 6:9 ESV

TRUTH FOR TODAY

Chronic difficult seasons
make me feel like I can't keep going,
but God will reward my persistence.

REFLECTION

When I feel like quitting,
I need to remind myself that God says . . .

AND WHEN YOU *draw close* TO GOD,

GOD WILL DRAW CLOSE *to you*.

WASH YOUR HANDS, YOU SINNERS,

AND LET YOUR *hearts* BE FILLED

WITH *God alone* TO MAKE THEM PURE

AND *true to Him*.

JAMES 4:8 TLB

ACTIVITY

Turn the word *STAND* into an acronym choosing positive, hopeful words or phrases.

EXAMPLE

S: Strong
T: Thrive
A: Anticipate
N: Never give up
D: Determined

Your turn.

S ______________________________

T ______________________________

A ______________________________

N ______________________________

D ______________________________

Tomorrow's Forecast

You can't have a better tomorrow
if you're thinking about yesterday all of the time.
CHARLES KETTERING

Remember that scene in *The Wizard of Oz* where Professor Marvel claims to see the future? He leads Dorothy to believe that Auntie Em is going to mourn her loss if she goes away. Seeing into the future changes Dorothy's mind about running away, and she turns around and goes back home to the farm.

Rather than using a crystal ball, it's better just to trust in God and not try to predict what's coming. You can guess all day long, but knowing how things will work out? Well, that's only for the Lord to know.

Bonnie wished she had a crystal ball. After she and her husband applied for a mortgage, they waited . . . and waited . . . and waited. The days dragged on, minutes feeling like hours. Either the mortgage company was slow in responding or the news wasn't going to be good. She feared they wouldn't qualify. Or maybe they would. Yes, surely with their recent income increase, they were good candidates. Back and forth she went in her mind, trying to guess the future.

AFFIRMATION

I don't know what tomorrow holds, but I know Who holds tomorrow.

"Not knowing" was the hardest part of all. Bonnie nearly made herself sick in the days leading up to the news. Only when she got the "You're in!" call from her lender did she breathe a sigh of relief. Why did she fret? She should have just trusted God all along.

The Lord would prefer we not get ourselves worked up in a lather while we're waiting. The goal is to be at peace, even when we don't know the outcome. It's not easy, but when we learn to live like that, we're not knotted up in anxiety all the time.

One thing is for sure: God is in our tomorrows. We can't see Him, but He has already gone ahead of us. So you can rest assured the future will be bright, because He's already there.

GOD SAYS

"Therefore do not worry about tomorrow,
for tomorrow will worry about itself.
Each day has enough trouble of its own."

MATTHEW 6:34 NIV

TRUTH FOR TODAY

I should focus on today, not tomorrow.
God's got it all under control.

REFLECTION

When I'm tempted to worry
about what tomorrow will look like,
I remember God's promise that . . .

Trust IN THE LORD
WITH *all your heart,*
AND *do not* LEAN ON
your own UNDERSTANDING.

PROVERBS 3:5 ESV

ACTIVITY

A letter from my eight-year-old self.

Dear ___________,

The year is ___________ and things have really changed! Remember when you were young and you used to worry about ___________,

and ___________?

Boy, did God ever turn those things around! He proved Himself faithful in every circumstance once you decided to stand strong. Your ___________ grew stronger and your ___________ got you through. If I could leave you with one piece of advice, it would be this: ___________.

Trust in God. He will never let you down—I promise!

Hang in there!

The Courage to Be Imperfect

We don't have to allow failure
to prevent us from being used by God.

ROBERT McGEE

Mary Poppins claimed to be "practically perfect in every way." (Somewhat immodest, right?) Most folks these days feel the need to be perfect, just like Mary. Usually this starts when we're in our teens as we try to look like, dress like, and act like all the others. It doesn't get much better after we marry or head into our occupations. We still fight the temptation to fit in by being just like our peers, especially the perfect ones.

If only our hair was fashionable like that.

If only we could go back to childhood and change one little thing.

If only we could find a better job.

If only we said the right thing at the right time like our practically perfect friend always did . . . and so on.

The comparison game becomes a daily struggle if we're not careful to guard our hearts.

This is especially true when we spend time on social media, where everyone puts their best face forward. If their posts are to be believed, our friends really are pictures of perfection, both on the job and at home. Wow! How did they get the golden ticket and all you got was the dog who drools on the furniture and the kids who leave their dirty socks on the floor?

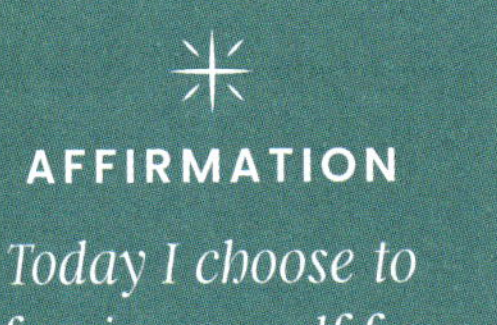

Here's a fun fact: no one is perfect. Romans 3:10 (NIV) says, "There is no one righteous, not even one." So all those practically-perfect-in-every-way friends? They're not. Not even close.

Today, take the time to forgive yourself for the mistakes you've made. The flaws. The imperfections. The mess-ups. The mix-ups. Forgive yourself. And remember, there's only One who is perfect, and He thinks you're pretty amazing just as you are.

GOD SAYS

*"You must not be envious of your neighbor's house,
or want to sleep with his wife,
or want to own his slaves, oxen, donkeys,
or anything else he has."*

EXODUS 20:17 TLB

TRUTH FOR TODAY

Envy is tempting. But I can get rid
of the green-eyed monster with God's help.

REFLECTION

Acknowledging jealousy is going to be hard,
but I know that . . .

THERE IS *no one* RIGHTEOUS,

NOT EVEN ONE.

ROMANS 3:10 NIV

ACTIVITY

Each circle below represents the person, place, and/or thing you're jealous of. Identify each, then color the circles in various shades of green—lightest to darkest, depending on the depth of your envy. Afterward, pray over each one and ask God to help you let it go.

Memory Bank Deposits

Each day of our lives we make deposits in the memory banks of our children.

CHARLES SWINDOLL

"I have the best idea ever!" Deena said. "When you turn thirteen, I'm going to take you to Paris!"

"Really, Mom?" Nine-year-old Peyton let out a squeal. "Ooh-la-la! I love Paris!"

Deena set up a special account for the trip and started putting money into it. Unfortunately, after her divorce, the money in that account had to be used to pay for their move to a different house. And before she knew it, Peyton was about to turn thirteen. There would be no trip to Paris, but how could she tell her daughter?

But when Deena gave Peyton the news, the nearly-thirteen-year-old surprised her with, "I have an idea, Mom. Let's do a Paris-themed party. I saw a picture online. It will be easy and fun and not very expensive."

Deena hated that she had to add the "not very expensive" part but appreciated her daughter's thoughtfulness. Maybe one day they really would go to Paris. But for now, she would focus on planning the best Paris-themed birthday party any thirteen-year-old ever had.

AFFIRMATION

I will make deposits into the memory banks of those I love on a regular basis!

Maybe you've been there. You had grand ideas. Then the realities of your singleness kicked in and you realized you had to let that kiddo down. Again.

It's devastating not to be able to follow through, but sometimes you have no choice. When it comes to a choice between paying the rent or doing something fun with the kids, the rent comes first.

But that doesn't mean you can't plan fun experiences. Instead of going to Paris, France, go to Paris, Texas! (If you live in Texas, of course.) Instead of tickets to the big ball game, plan a ball-themed party at the house with cupcakes that look like baseballs.

You get the idea. You can make your kids' days bright, despite any circumstances you're walking through. Use your imagination, and you'll come up with reasonably priced ideas in no time.

GOD SAYS

One generation shall commend your works to another,
and shall declare your mighty acts.

PSALM 145:4 ESV

TRUTH FOR TODAY

I can make deposits into others' memory banks
by taking the time to invest in their lives,
one person at a time.

REFLECTION

When I think about the people
with whom I would like to create memories,
I think about . . .

THE ONE WHO *blesses others*

IS *abundantly* BLESSED;

THOSE WHO *help others* ARE HELPED.

PROVERBS 11:25 THE MESSAGE

ACTIVITY

Whom would you like to invest in?
Write a plan to leave a memory a loved one can enjoy.

From the Bank of

____

DATE ______________________

PAY TO THE ORDER OF ______________________

____

MEMORY BANK IDEA ______________________

____

____

____

____

____

SIGNED ______________________

Hopscotching Along

Life is not about how fast you run or how high you climb, but how well you bounce.

VIVIAN KOMORI

Remember playing hopscotch as a kid? You would start with a stellar chalk drawing on the driveway. Then you tossed a stone into a square and started hopping—only on one foot, unless the numbers lined up just right. Only then could you put that second foot down.

It's not always easy to keep your balance, especially if you're moving fast, but that's half the fun! You're testing your agility, after all.

The game of hopscotch dates back to thousands of years ago, when Roman soldiers would play to increase their speed and their amazing strength. Back in those days, they would hop along the length of a hundred feet while carrying large weights. Whew!

AFFIRMATION

Tomorrow will be better. Until then, I'll lean on the Holy Spirit and follow His lead.

Maybe you feel like those soldiers some days. You're loaded down with cares—hop, hop, hopping along, praying you can keep your balance. Are you getting enough sleep? Are you eating right? Do the kids have enough of your attention? Did you feed the dog? Did you pay the mortgage? Is there enough food in the pantry to cook a proper meal this evening? Do you need to go shopping? Would fast food (again!) be a problem?

Talk about a balancing act!

Some days you just can't stay inside the lines, no matter how hard you try. You land far outside the safe boundaries. You end up yelling at the kids, fighting with your best friend, or getting irritated at your boss. Hey, it happens!

On days like that, remember to solidify your stance by spending time with the Lord. When you're out of balance, He's as steady as a rock! And don't ever forget, the Holy Spirit isn't just your Comforter; He's also your Guide. He'll keep you moving into many bright tomorrows if you keep your focus on Him and not on the agility course in front of you.

GOD SAYS

Look carefully then how you walk,
not as unwise but as wise,
making the best use of the time,
because the days are evil.
Therefore do not be foolish,
but understand what the will of the Lord is.

EPHESIANS 5:15–17 ESV

TRUTH FOR TODAY

I can keep things in balance
if I stick to God's plan
and guard my time with Him.

REFLECTION

When things get out of balance, I need to . . .

LET US NOT BECOME WEARY IN *doing good,*

FOR AT THE PROPER TIME WE WILL *reap*

a harvest IF WE DO NOT GIVE UP.

GALATIANS 6:9 NIV

ACTIVITY

Do you feel like you're hopscotching through life, moving from activity to activity? Write down the areas of your life that are hard to keep in balance, then pray over each one.

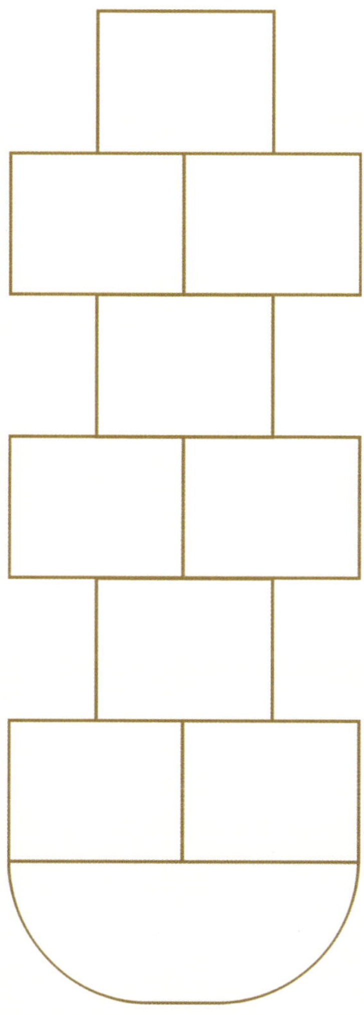

When the Bough Breaks

At sunset the little soul that had come with the dawning went away, leaving heartbreak behind it.

L. M. MONTGOMERY

The world stopped spinning on the day Lynn got the news. She went in for a routine OB/GYN visit to check on baby Evie's growth. Well into her fourth month, the baby girl should be growing like a weed.

The doctor put the scope on Lynn's belly but couldn't find Evie's heartbeat. After several failed attempts, Lynn was sent in for an ultrasound, where the horrifying news was confirmed.

Evie didn't make it.

Lynn fell apart at the seams. Everything she and her husband had dreamed of . . . watching her take her first step, say her first word, growing up . . . all gone. In an instant. The baby girl they had named, cherished, and joyously proclaimed as their own . . . no more.

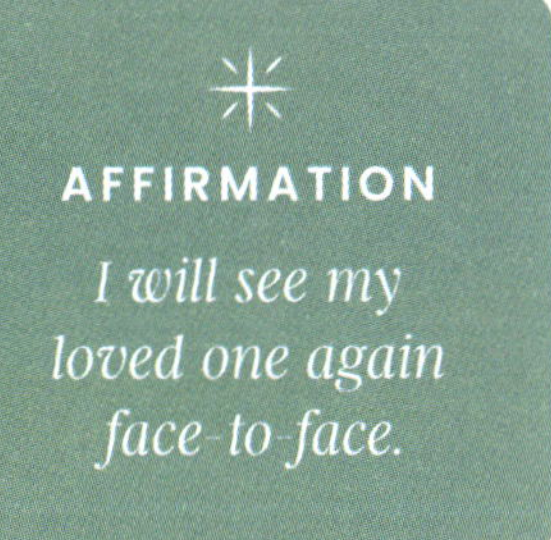

After the sobbing stopped, all that was left was a sick, empty feeling, like nothing Lynn had ever experienced before. She wondered if the pain would ever leave or if she would feel like this forever.

Maybe you know Lynn's gut-wrenching pain all too well. You've been in her position. You've lost a child or a close loved one. And your world was rocked as never before. Shock. Disappointment. Grief. Emptiness. You felt it all. And, at the same time, you felt nothing. The sun kept shining, but you wished it wouldn't. People kept sending texts and cards, but you had nothing to say in response. And God? Where was He?

It's hard to picture "brighter days ahead" when you've lost everything. Seems impossible. And it's a cruel time for people to remind you that you'll "just get over it." You won't. Ever. But the Holy Spirit—over a passage of time—will ease the pain you're feeling and replace it with longing to see that precious face one day.

You will, you know. Your loved one will be waiting for you in heaven, where all the days ahead will be radiantly beautiful and you will spend them together.

GOD SAYS

He will wipe away every tear from their eyes,
and death shall be no more,
neither shall there be mourning, nor crying, nor pain anymore,
for the former things have passed away.

REVELATION 21:4 ESV

TRUTH FOR TODAY

God is in the business of healing broken hearts and lives.

REFLECTION

Grief can feel like a deep, dark tunnel
from which I'll never emerge, but with God . . .

BROTHERS AND SISTERS, WE DO NOT WANT YOU TO BE *uninformed* ABOUT THOSE WHO SLEEP IN DEATH, SO THAT YOU DO NOT GRIEVE LIKE THE REST OF MANKIND, WHO HAVE *no hope.* FOR WE BELIEVE THAT *Jesus died* AND *rose again,* AND SO WE BELIEVE THAT GOD *will bring with Jesus those who have fallen asleep* IN HIM.

I THESSALONIANS 4:13–14 NIV

ACTIVITY

On a separate piece of paper, cut out a large heart and then tear it into pieces. On each piece, write down one heartache you've experienced. Then, tape the pieces of the heart back together, turn it over, and write the words "Healed and Whole" on the back. Tape it here.

Is There More?

Sometimes, the smallest things
take up the most room in your heart.

A. A. MILNE

"I don't know. I'm just feeling . . ." Dana paced the room, trying to think of the right word. "Discontent. I mean, I have a good life, but there are days when I feel like I'm going through the motions. I work long hours, then I come home and cook and clean. I fall into bed. Then I start all over again the next day. Sometimes I wonder if it's all for nothing. I hardly have time to spend with Kevin or the kids."

AFFIRMATION

I won't get hung up on how many hours I spend with my loved ones. I'll just make them the best hours possible!

"I remember feeling that way when you were little, Dana," her mother responded.

"What am I working for, anyway, if not to give them a better life? How is being away from them so much a better life?"

"Can I ask you a question, honey?" her mom asked. "Do you feel like you had a good childhood?"

"Me?" Dana couldn't help but smile. "The best! We lived in a great house in an awesome school district. I loved our church and our neighborhood. And remember those great road trips we used to take? I loved all of that."

"Mm-hmm." Her mom paused. "Don't you see? I was working full-time just like you are now. But you're not remembering what you missed out on. You're only remembering the things Dad and I managed to pack into the hours when we were all together. So don't feel too bad about your schedule. God will show you how to prioritize to give the kids adequate time. They'll come away with great memories too."

Maybe you can relate to Dana's plight. It feels like your life is all work and no play, with little time left over for others. Perhaps it's time to put a plan in motion for an upcoming trip or a vacation with your hubby or close friend. As you look toward the future with those you love, you'll be reminded that there is certainly more to your existence than just work.

GOD SAYS

Keep your life free from love of money,
and be content with what you have,
for he has said, "I will never leave you nor forsake you."

HEBREWS 13:5 ESV

TRUTH FOR TODAY

God is with me no matter what,
so I can be content with what I have.

REFLECTION

Instead of fretting over all the things I don't have,
I can shift my focus by . . .

AND MY GOD WILL SUPPLY

all your needs ACCORDING TO

HIS RICHES IN GLORY *in Christ Jesus.*

PHILIPPIANS 4:19 NASB

ACTIVITY

If you could only own four things, what would they be?
Sketch/write/tape photos of them here.
Then ask God to help you be content whether you have them or not.

EXAMPLES

Your Worth Is in Him

Your value doesn't decrease based on someone else's inability to see your worth.

UNKNOWN

Rhonda had flown under the radar much of her life. There were plenty of other people more talented, more boisterous, or more spiritual. Whenever she compared herself to them, she often wondered if she had anything to offer. Rhonda wanted to play softball in high school, and she did her best at try-outs, but she didn't get picked for the team. When the choir director asked her to audition for the spring show at her school, she sang her favorite song but didn't get picked. She ended up working in the tech department backstage. Rhonda really enjoyed the experience and did her best, though she got no applause like the people onstage.

AFFIRMATION

Today I ask for God's vision, that I might see myself as He does.

When she got to college, Rhonda excelled and ended up graduating at the top of her class. Her parents gave her a few pats on the back but nothing more.

When she got married, Rhonda's husband wasn't the kind who would gush over how pretty she looked or how well she kept the house, though she gave her best shot at both. After a while, Rhonda wondered if others saw any worth in her at all.

Maybe you're a Rhonda. You're wondering, even now, why people seem to see right past you. They don't notice your talents or abilities.

Oh, but there is One who does notice, and He thinks you're a woman of many talents! He planted those gifts and abilities inside of you and has been there all along, stirring them up. And He will place you in just the right place at the right time to use them.

Does it matter if you don't get the applause or accolades? Sure, it would be nice to have those things from time to time. But even if it doesn't come from those around you, just picture your heavenly Father cheering you on as you do what He made you to do!

GOD SAYS

"Are not five sparrows sold for two pennies?
And not one of them is forgotten before God.
Why, even the hairs of your head are all numbered.
Fear not; you are of more value than many sparrows."

LUKE 12:6–7 ESV

TRUTH FOR TODAY

If God finds value in the birds of the air,
then surely He finds even more value in me.

REFLECTION

When feelings of unworthiness creep up,
I can always . . .

WHATEVER YOU DO, *work heartily,*
as for the Lord AND NOT FOR MEN,
KNOWING THAT FROM THE LORD YOU WILL
receive the inheritance AS YOUR REWARD.
YOU ARE SERVING *the Lord Christ.*

COLOSSIANS 3:23–24 ESV

ACTIVITY

What video loop plays in your head, convincing you you're unworthy? Write it down and then pray for the video to stop playing.

THE MOVIE IN MY MIND

Scars or Stars?

Being in Christ, it is safe to forget the past;
it is possible to be sure of the future;
it is possible to be diligent in the present.

ALEXANDER MACLAREN

Meredith was diagnosed with skin cancer when she was in her forties. The spot was awkwardly placed on her face, just to the left of her nose. The plastic surgeon decided that a small surgery would be necessary, one that would require nearly a dozen stitches.

Meredith was mortified. What would she look like afterward? Would the scar be prominent, or could she cover it with makeup once the spot healed?

It took several weeks for the surgery site—close to two inches long—to heal and for a scar to form. Fortunately, the surgeon had done an excellent job with his stitches, and the resulting scar wasn't terribly prominent after all. Still, it was the first thing she noticed whenever she glanced in the mirror. Was it the first thing others saw too?

Maybe you feel scarred like Meredith. The scars might not be on the outside, visible to a watching world, but you've been scarred by the pain you've experienced. The situations that hurt you the most have left their marks. And you're worried those scars are visible to others.

AFFIRMATION

I will never refuse to see the stars, no matter how big my scars.

It's time to change the way you think about those scars. Could you begin to see them as what they are . . . stars? They are, you know, for they are a reminder, not of the pain, but of the proof that you overcame that situation.

Meredith's doctor got all that cancer out when he performed surgery, and it never returned. She was able to relax and look forward to brighter days ahead because she didn't have that "What if?" hanging over her head.

You can relax too. You're an overcomer. And God is going to take the scars of yesterday and turn them into the stars of tomorrow if you trust Him to do so.

GOD SAYS

Every good and perfect gift is from above,
coming down from the Father of the heavenly lights,
who does not change like shifting shadows.

JAMES 1:17 NIV

TRUTH FOR TODAY

May I always express gratitude
to the Giver of all good gifts.

REFLECTION

When I stop to think about
all I have to be grateful for, I . . .

WE KNOW THAT *in all things* GOD WORKS FOR *the good* OF THOSE WHO *love Him*, WHO HAVE BEEN *called* ACCORDING TO *His purpose.*

ROMANS 8:28 NIV

ACTIVITY

Let's play Bingo! Put an X through each square as you fulfill it.

Tell a friend why you're grateful for him/her.	Share your favorite food with someone.	Express gratitude for you occupation/ income.	Thank the person who taught you the skill you are most grateful for.	Lend the book you are most grateful for to someone.
Express gratitude to your grandparent, parent, or child.	Make a note of the moment you are most grateful for today.	Describe the scent you are most grateful for.	Document a family tradition you are grateful for with family.	What technology are you most grateful for?
Share the song you are most grateful for on social media or text.	Describe the holiday you are most grateful for.	**FREE SPACE**	Thank the person who gave you the knowledge you are most grateful for.	Tell your pastors why you are grateful for them.
Explain to a custodian or other service provider why you are grateful for him/her.	Describe a person who made you think bigger.	Describe a day that changed your course for which you are grateful.	Show a soldier, veteran, or first responder your gratitude.	Draw or photograph the thing in nature you are most grateful to have seen.
Tell a waiter, cashier, or server how grateful you are for their service.	Find out more about the place you are most grateful to have visited/lived.	Describe the difficult situation you are grateful to have overcome.	Describe the season you are most grateful for.	Tell a sibling or family member why you are grateful for him/her.

One Step at a Time

A hero is an ordinary individual who finds the strength to persevere and endure in spite of overwhelming obstacles.

CHRISTOPHER REEVE

After an accident that broke her tibia and fibula, Jenny had to undergo surgery for the bones to be pinned and plated back together. She spent several days in the hospital and then another few days in a rehab hospital.

Finally free to go home in a wheelchair, she faced an unexpected challenge. Jenny lived alone in a two-story townhome with her bedroom upstairs and the living area downstairs. She planned to spend her daytime hours downstairs so that she could let her two dogs in and out, but how would she get up to the second floor at night? And once she got there, how would she manage getting down the hallway to her room?

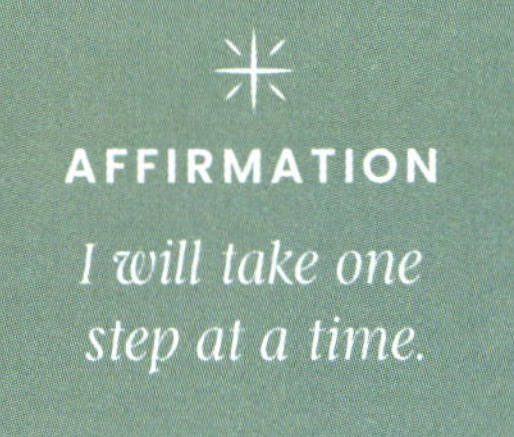

A plan came to her, one that just might work. She needed the help of a friend to implement it for the first time, but her friend was happy to oblige. Jenny rolled her wheelchair to the foot of the stairs and scooted out. She sat backward on the stairs and then—one at a time—eased her way up until she finally reached the top of the stairs. Once there, she managed to get into the rolling office chair her friend had strategically placed. Then she rolled across the wooden floor to her bedroom. Perfect! Worked like a charm.

We can get pretty creative when we have to, right? But scooting up the stairs on your backside? That's not something you ever think you'll have to do.

There are situations, however, when you have no choice but to move one step at a time. The situation seems too overwhelming otherwise. You think to yourself, "There's just no way. I'll never make it through this."

One foot in front of the other, sister. Tomorrow is waiting with open arms, but only if you take steps in that direction (even if they're small ones).

GOD SAYS

Therefore, since we are surrounded by so great a cloud of witnesses, let us also lay aside every weight, and sin which clings so closely, and let us run with endurance the race that is set before us.

HEBREWS 12:1 ESV

TRUTH FOR TODAY

When I feel like giving up, I'll draw encouragement from the stories of the great people of the Bible.

REFLECTION

When I start to feel sorry for myself, I will remember favorite Bible stories like the one . . .

THEREFORE, SINCE WE ARE SURROUNDED

BY SO GREAT A CLOUD OF WITNESSES,

LET US ALSO *lay aside* EVERY WEIGHT,

AND SIN WHICH CLINGS SO CLOSELY,

AND LET US *run with endurance*

the race THAT IS SET BEFORE US.

HEBREWS 12:1 ESV

ACTIVITY

There are situations when you have no choice but to move one step at a time. The situation seems too overwhelming otherwise. Choose which step will get you through the day. Some days you may need to take every step.

TODAY I WILL:

A. Eat a gallon of ice cream

B. Call my best friend

C. Pray through my situation

D. All of the above

I WILL FIND STRENGTH TO PERSEVERE:

A. By building my physical muscles

B. By building my spiritual muscles

C. By binge-watching my favorite TV show

D. By eating a gallon of ice cream

E. All of the above

I CAN DRAW FROM:

A. Past experiences

B. My pea-sized faith

C. People of faith around me

D. All of the above

BIBLE CHARACTERS WHOSE STORIES CHEER ME ON:

A. Moses

B. David

C. Hannah

D. All of the above

The Courage to Show Up (Hey, You Showed Up!)

Courage doesn't always roar.
Sometimes courage is the quiet voice
at the end of the day saying,
"I will try again tomorrow."

MARY ANNE RADMACHER

Hey, you. Yes, you! The one who's been so hung up on your struggles that moving forward has been difficult. You've come a long way, baby! No, really. Think of how much braver you've gotten over the years. The things that used to frighten you? They're no big deal now. The things that used to keep you awake at night? You hardly think about them anymore. You're tougher now and better able to face the future without all the trembling.

Oh, I know, you don't see yourself that way, but you've made a lot of progress lately. You're stronger, braver, and kinder too. You've tackled financial matters, housing issues, relationship woes, and even job-related chaos, and you've come through like a champ. You showed up for the hard moments. You showed up for the heartbreaking moments. You showed up in the muck and mire of the daily grind, and you learned from every terrible, horrible, no-good, very bad day that you're capable of more than you ever knew.

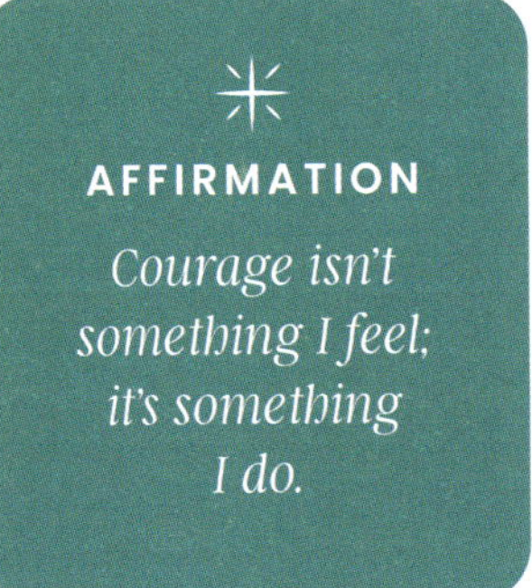

AFFIRMATION

Courage isn't something I feel; it's something I do.

Don't ever sell yourself short. With God on your side, you're a powerhouse! And when you're courageous, you're unstoppable!

So keep on showing up. And lead the way for children, friends, relatives, and fellow employees. People are looking to you. They're saying, "If she can do it, I can too."

So, do it.

Then keep doing it.

Then do it some more.

GOD SAYS

But, as it is written, "What no eye has seen,
nor ear heard, nor the heart of man imagined,
what God has prepared for those who love him"—
these things God has revealed to us through the Spirit.
For the Spirit searches everything,
even the depths of God.

I CORINTHIANS 2:9–10 ESV

TRUTH FOR TODAY

I can bravely step through the doors of opportunity because God's Spirit goes before me.

REFLECTION

I know that God is the great door opener, which is why I . . .

FOR I CAN DO *everything*

GOD ASKS ME TO

WITH *the help of Christ*

WHO GIVES ME THE *strength* AND *power.*

PHILIPPIANS 4:13 TLB

ACTIVITY

The door of opportunity.

WHAT'S HOLDING YOU BACK FROM STEPPING THROUGH THE DOOR OF OPPORTUNITY?

WHAT COULD HAPPEN IF YOU COURAGEOUSLY STEPPED THROUGH?

Hope in the Hard: Interactive Inspirational Journal

First Edition, July 2025

Published by:

21154 Highway 16 East
Siloam Springs, AR 72761
dayspring.com

Written by: Janice Thompson
Designed by: Lauren Purtle

Printed in Vietnam
Prime: U3087
ISBN: 979-8-88602-927-7